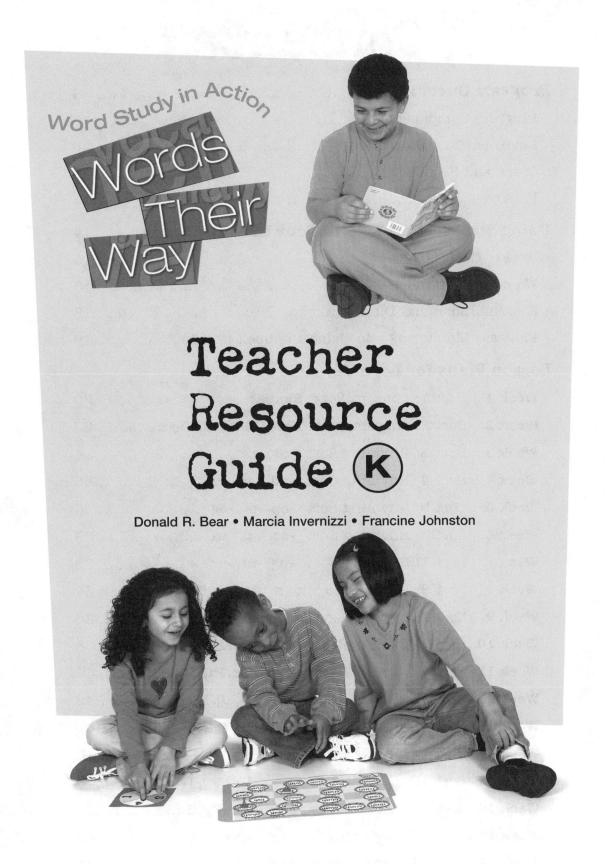

Word Study in Action

Words Their Way

Teacher Resource Guide Ⓚ

Donald R. Bear • Marcia Invernizzi • Francine Johnston

CELEBRATION PRESS

Pearson Learning Group

# Contents

## Program Reviewers

Pam Brown, Teacher
Sayre School
Lexington, KY

Katrina Currier, Language Arts Curriculum Coordinator
San Francisco Day School
San Francisco, CA

Kathy Lamkin, Teacher
Tuscan Elementary School
Maplewood, NJ

Shellie Winter, Teacher
Ponce de Leon Elementary School
Clearwater, FL

The following people have contributed to the development of this product:
*Art and Design:* Tricia Battipede, Sherri Hieber-Day, Dorothea Fox, Denise Ingrassia, David Mager, Judy Mahoney, Elbaliz Mendez
*Editorial:* Leslie Feierstone-Barna, Linette Mathewson, Tracey Randinelli
*Inventory:* Yvette Higgins
*Marketing:* Christine Fleming
*Production/Manufacturing:* Alan Dalgleish
*Publishing Operations:* Jennifer Van Der Heide

ISBN 0-7652-6700-4

Printed in the United States of America
8 9 10     08

Celebration Press
Pearson Learning Group

**1-800-321-3106**
**www.pearsonlearning.com**

# Program Overview

Teachers have been using *Words Their Way: Word Study for Phonics, Vocabulary, and Spelling Instruction* (Merrill/Prentice Hall, 1996, 2000, 2004), authored by noted researchers Donald R. Bear, Marcia Invernizzi, Francine Johnston, and Shane Templeton, to teach children phonics, spelling, and vocabulary for the past eight years. This powerful approach to word study teaches children to look closely at words to discover the regularities and conventions of English orthography needed to read and spell. The success of this instruction has led Pearson Learning Group to publish *Words Their Way: Word Study in Action*, the official companion, in a ready-to-use format. This multi-component curriculum helps children increase their knowledge of the spelling patterns and the meanings of specific words and generalize this knowledge to the English spelling system.

## How Does Words Their Way: Word Study in Action Work?

The heart of the *Words Their Way: Word Study in Action* program is the **sort**, or the process of grouping sounds, words, and pictures that represent words into specific categories. Word sorting includes teacher-directed instruction as well as independent learning. You begin by demonstrating how to sort picture or word cards by sound or pattern. Later, as children sort word cards or picture cards on their own, they make discoveries and generalizations about the conventions of English orthography. They compare and contrast word features and discover similarities and differences within the categories.

*Words Their Way: Word Study in Action* consists of 36 sorts in Levels K, B, and C, and 38 sorts in Level A. Each sort is designed to be completed in a week. The sequence of the program is based on the alphabet, pattern, and meaning principles that have been observed in children's spelling. *Words Their Way: Word Study in Action* provides the following important hands-on experiences:

- Comparing and contrasting words by sound so that children can categorize similar sounds and associate them consistently with letters and letter combinations. For example, words spelled with -*at* (*rat, sat, fat*) are compared with words spelled with -*ot* (*not, lot, rot*).
- Comparing and contrasting words by consistent spelling patterns associated with categories of sound. For example, words spelled with -*oi* (*join, soil, coin*) are compared with words spelled with -*oy* (*joy, annoy, coy*).
- Categorizing words by meaning, use, and parts of speech

# Words Their Way: Word Study in Action and "Reading First"

In April 2000, the National Reading Panel (NRP) issued a report describing how children learn to read. As an offshoot of that report, and as part of No Child Left Behind (NCLB), the Reading First (RF) initiative was established. Reading First focuses on five areas of reading instruction needed to successfully teach children to read—phonemic awareness, phonics, fluency, comprehension, and vocabulary. *Words Their Way: Word Study in Action* addresses these five essential reading components in the following ways:

**Phonemic awareness:** Children identify picture names that begin with the same sound, isolate and say the first sound in picture names, identify and categorize onsets and rhymes, and build words by substituting consonant sounds and blending them with various word families.

**Phonics:** Children sort words by beginning and ending consonants, consonant blends or digraphs, CVC short-vowel rhyming families, and long vowel patterns. They learn to analyze letter-sound relationships and how to use spelling patterns to decode words in reading and spell words in writing.

**Fluency:** Children listen as you model fluent reading of poems and books that contains the phonics elements they are learning and leads to fluency in letter and word recognition.

**Comprehension:** Children learn to read words quickly and accurately through word study so they are empowered to read with greater understanding.

**Vocabulary:** Children learn the meanings of words by sorting them according to categories, such as living and nonliving things. Words are categorized by meaning and parts of speech.

## About the Authors

**Donald R. Bear** is director of the E. L. Cord Center for Learning and Literacy in the College of Education at the University of Nevada, Reno. He teaches in the literacy center and meets with schools and districts to plan literacy programs. He is a former preschool and elementary teacher whose recent research includes the study of literacy development in different languages.

**Marcia Invernizzi** is a professor of reading education at the Curry School of Education at the University of Virginia. She is also the director of the McGuffey Reading Center, where she teaches the clinical practica in diagnosis and remediation, doctoral seminars in reading research, and a course in word study. She is formerly an English and reading teacher and is the principal author of Phonological Awareness Literacy Screening (PALS).

**Francine Johnston** is an associate professor at the School of Education at the University of North Carolina at Greensboro, where she teaches courses in reading, language arts, and children's literature. She taught in public schools for sixteen years as a first grade teacher and reading specialist. Her research interests include the relationship between spelling and reading achievement.

# Program Components

*Words Their Way: Word Study in Action* supports the routines established in *Words Their Way: Word Study for Phonics, Vocabulary, and Spelling Instruction* by providing the materials you need for each sort in a ready-to-use format. Picture and word cards, sorting grids, game boards, and reading materials that contain the same spelling patterns and vocabulary they sorted are all provided.

*Words Their Way: Word Study in Action* contains the following components:

Each level of the program (K, A, B, C) features a consumable **Word Study Notebook**. The Word Study Notebook contains a four-page lesson for each sort, including picture and/or word cards for children to cut out and a grid onto which children sort and paste the picture/word cards. Each lesson also contains a written activity that gives children practice in the skill that corresponds to the lesson's sort. The letter to families on the inside front cover of the Word Study Notebook connects classroom word-study work with practice at home, promoting family involvement. An **envelope** is provided for children to store their picture/word cards for the week. A convenient self-stick strip allows the envelope to be attached to the inside back cover of the Word Study Notebook.

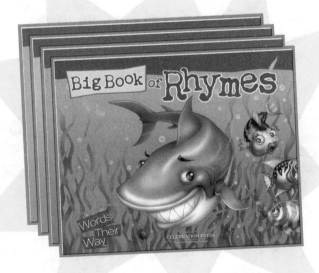

The **Big Book of Rhymes**, included with Levels K, A, and B of *Words Their Way: Word Study in Action*, contains a poem for each lesson. Words in the poems reflect the skill covered in the corresponding sort. High-interest, engaging illustrations accompany each poem and can be used to foster discussion.

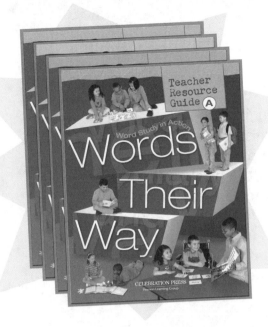

All four levels of *Words Their Way: Word Study in Action* feature a **Teacher Resource Guide**, containing lesson plans for each sort in the level, along with an explanation of how to use the program and tips for progress monitoring and classroom management.

The **Teacher Resource CD** is an interactive resource provided with all four levels of *Words Their Way: Word Study in Action*. The CD-ROM contains a variety of materials that can be printed and integrated into classroom word-study instruction:

- **Picture/word cards** can be used to demonstrate each sort in a level.

- **Games and activities** give children additional practice in each week's sort skill.

- **Build, Blend, and Extend activities** in Levels K and A focus on building new words and blending word parts for additional phonics, phonemic awareness, and word-study practice.

- **Sorts** from the last half of the previous level and the first half of the next level help you address the needs of children who may require extra practice or who may be ready for more challenging material.

- **Blank templates** allow you and your students to create your own sorts and games.

Most sorts in Levels K, A, B, and C are aligned to corresponding little books from the ***Words Their Way* Library.** Each book features a skill covered in the week's sort. Stories are age-appropriate and appealing.

An optional **storage box** with labeled file folders lets you organize all of the materials for each sort, as well as your copy of the Word Study Notebook and the Teacher Resource Guide.

# Developmental Stages

The methodology of *Words Their Way: Word Study for Phonics, Vocabulary, and Spelling Instruction* reflects a progression of stages that describe children's spelling behavior as they move from one level of word knowledge to the next. The stages cited in the book make it easier to understand and recognize the basic strategies that children use to spell. In *Words Their Way: Word Study in Action*, these stages have been adapted to correspond to specific levels within the program. Levels K, A, B, and C of *Words Their Way: Word Study in Action* cover four spelling stages: Emergent, Letter Name-Alphabetic, Within Word Pattern, and Syllables and Affixes.

**Emergent Spelling (Level K/On-level Kindergarten)** During this stage, children learn to recognize and write the letters of the alphabet. They play with the sounds in words and letters. Most of the sound play focuses on beginning and rhyming sounds. Through most of Level K, children sort pictures by rhyme and beginning sounds. By the end of the level, children acquire an understanding of the concept of words and begin to match picture cards to the words that represent their names.

**Letter Name-Alphabetic Spelling (Level A/On-level Grade 1)** At the beginning of this stage, children apply the alphabet principles primarily to consonants. By the end of the stage, children are able to represent most short vowel patterns, consonant digraphs, and consonant blends correctly. In Level A, children sort pictures and/or words by beginning consonants, digraphs, and blends, and by word families.

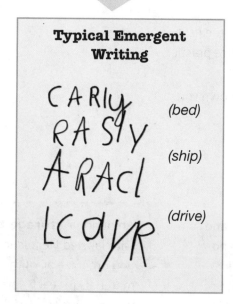

### Typical Emergent Writing

CARIy (bed)

RASIy (ship)

ARACl (drive)

LCdYR

### Typical Letter Name-Alphabetic Spelling

BAD for *bed*
SEP or SHP for *ship*
FOT for *float*
LOP for *lump*

| Examples | Emergent (Level K) |
|---|---|
| bed | |
| ship | |
| float | |
| train | |
| cattle | |
| cellar | |

**Within Word Pattern Spelling (Level B/On-level Grade 2)** Children at the beginning of this stage spell most single-syllable, short vowel words correctly. Then children move away from the sound-by-sound approach of the letter name and begin to include patterns or chunks of letter sequences that relate to sound and meaning. In Level B, children begin to sort words by long vowel patterns.

**Syllables and Affixes Spelling (Level C/On-level Grade 3)** By this stage, children already spell most one-syllable short and long vowel words correctly. The focus of instruction shifts to multisyllabic words and patterns. In *Words Their Way: Word Study in Action*, children sort Level C words by specific vowel combinations, inflected endings (including plurals, *-ing*, and *-ed*), and vowel patterns in accented syllables.

| Typical Within Word Pattern Spelling |
|---|
| TRANE for train |
| SOPE for soap |
| DRIEV for drive |
| SPOLE for spoil |

| Typical Syllables and Affixes Spelling |
|---|
| SELLER for *cellar* |
| DAMIGE for *damage* |
| RIDDING for *riding* |
| FUNY for *funny* |

# Stages of Spelling in *Words Their Way*

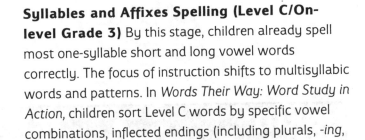

| Letter Name-Alphabetic (Level A) | | | | | Within Word Pattern (Level B) | | | | Syllables and Affixes (Level C) | | | |
|---|---|---|---|---|---|---|---|---|---|---|---|---|
| b bd | bad | | | | bed | | | | | | | |
| s sp | sep | shep | | | ship | | | | | | | |
| f ft | fot | flot | flott | | flowt | floaut | flote | float | | | | |
| t trn | jran | tan | chran | tran | teran | traen | trane | train | | | | |
| c kd | catl | | cadol | | | catel | catol | | cattel | cattle | | |
| s slr | salr | | celr | | | saler | celer | | seler | celler | seller | cellar |

9

# Scope and Sequence

The following chart shows the skills presented in *Words Their Way: Word Study in Action*. The first column lists the skills. The subsequent columns indicate the *Words Their Way* level or levels at which the skills are covered.

| Skill | Level K | Level A | Level B | Level C |
|---|---|---|---|---|
| Concept Sorts | • | | | |
| Rhyming Sorts | • | | | |
| Concepts of Word in Print | • | | | |
| Letter Recognition | • | | | |
| Beginning Sounds | • | | | |
| Ending Sounds **t, x** | • | | | |
| Short Vowels **a, e, i, o, u** | • | • | • | |
| Short Vowel Word Families | • | • | | |
| Beginning Consonants | | • | | |
| Consonant Digraphs | | • | • | |
| Consonant Blends | | • | • | |
| Beginning Sounds **k, wh, qu, tw** | | • | | |
| Short Vowel Words With Beginning Consonant Digraphs | | • | | |
| Short Vowel Words With Beginning Blends | | • | | |
| Short Vowel Words With Final Blends | | • | | |
| Long Vowels **a, e, i, o, u** | | • | • | |
| Final /k/ Sound Spelled **-ck, -ke,** or **-k** | | | • | |
| Consonant Digraphs With Short Vowels | | | • | |
| Consonant Digraphs With Long Vowels | | | • | |
| Consonant Digraphs Plus **r**-Blends and **squ** | | | • | |
| CVVC Patterns **ai, oa, ee, ea** | | | • | • |

| Skill | Level K | Level A | Level B | Level C |
|---|---|---|---|---|
| Diphthongs | | | • | • |
| Ambiguous Vowel Sounds | | | • | • |
| Long Vowel Patterns | | | • | • |
| r-Influenced Vowel Patterns | | | • | • |
| Silent Beginning Consonants **kn, wr, gn** | | | • | |
| Triple **r**-blends **scr, str, spr** | | | • | • |
| Vowel Digraphs | | | • | |
| Hard and Soft **c** and **g** | | | • | • |
| Word Endings **-ce, -ve, -se** | | | • | • |
| Word Endings **-dge, -ge** | | | | • |
| Word Endings **-tch, -ch** | | | | • |
| Homophones | | | | • |
| Contractions | | | | • |
| Plural Endings | | | | • |
| Inflected Endings **-ing** | | | | • |
| Inflected Endings **-ed** | | | | • |
| Unusual Past Tense Words | | | | • |
| Compound Words | | | | • |
| Syllable Juncture | | | | • |
| Open and Closed Syllables and Inflected Endings | | | | • |
| Long Vowel Patterns in Accented Syllables | | | | • |

# Research Base

With purposeful reading, writing, listening, and speaking, words are learned. Even more words are acquired when they are explicitly examined to discover relationships among sounds, spelling patterns, and meanings.

*Words Their Way: Word Study in Action* increases knowledge of the spelling patterns and the meaning of specific words. Children learn to compare, contrast, and classify categories of sounds and words.

| Research | Findings | Put Into Action With *Words Their Way* |
|---|---|---|
| Read, 1971, 1977 | • Students' spellings reveal systematic, phonetic logic underlying preschoolers' categorization of English speech sounds. | • Sorts focus on discovering similarities and differences in sounds, letters, letter-sounds, words, and meaning |
| Henderson, Estes, & Stonecash, 1972; Beers & Henderson, 1977; Gentry, 1980; Henderson, 1981 | • The spellings of primary school children reveal similar use of letter-name, alphabetic logic up to the next period of transition. | • Learning builds on what children know and what they are trying to negotiate. |
| Schlagal, 1982, 1986; Henderson & Templeton, 1986; Henderson, 1990; Invernizzi, Abouzeid & Gill, 1994 | • Developmental study of spelling in grades one through six reveals three discernable phases of orthographic understandings: alphabet, pattern, and meaning. | • Word study progresses through systematic instruction in sound, alphabetic letter-sound correspondences, spelling patterns, and spelling-meaning connections. |
| Morris & Perney, 1984; Bear, Truex, & Barone, 1989; Ganske, 1999 | • Developmental spelling analyses in the fall of the school year are reliable and valid predictors of literacy proficiency at the end of the school year. | • *Words Their Way* assessments place students in appropriate position in scope and sequence of *Words Their Way: Word Study in Action*. |
| Weber & Henderson, 1989; Hayes, 2004 | • Fourth grade students assigned to word sort group significantly outperform control group on standardized measures of reading and spelling. | • Students learn to recognize, decode, and write spelling patterns. |
| Ehri, 1997; Ellis, 1997; Perfetti, 1997; Perfetti, 2003 | • There is an interaction and integration of reading and spelling development. Students' orthographic knowledge develops in predictable phases. | • *Words Their Way: Word Study in Action* includes word study activities that are beneficial to both reading and spelling development at the best instructional level. |

| Research | Findings | Put Into Action With *Words Their Way* |
|---|---|---|
| Zutell & Rasinski, 1989; Johnston, 1998; Bear, 1992; Invernizzi, 1992; Templeton & Bear, 1992 | • Orthographic knowledge significantly predicts sight word acquisition, word recognition, and oral reading fluency. Relationships among spelling, reading, and writing are reciprocal and symbiotic. | • Students categorize words by sound, pattern, and meaning, then search for other words that work the same way in poems from the Big Book of Rhymes and books from the *Words Their Way* Library. Word recognition is enhanced when words are studied in isolation. |
| Worthy & Invernizzi, 1989; Sawyer, Lipa-Wade, Kim, Ritenour, & Knight, 1997; Cantrell, 1990, 1999; Bear, Templeton, Helman, & Baren, 2003 | • Children who have learning disabilities, speak nonstandard dialects, or are learning to read in different alphabetic languages demonstrate the same types of confusions. | • Alternate sorting activities and vocabulary building, alerts and instructions for English language learners, and teacher tips are provided with each week's work so the skills can be clarified, practiced, and extended. |
| Morris, Blanton, Blanton, Nowacek, & Perney, 1995; Hayes, 2004 | • Teaching low achieving spellers at their "instructional levels" yields greater gains than control group students who received grade-level instruction regardless of their instructional level. | • Ongoing spell checks allow for flexible grouping and differentiated phonics, spelling, and vocabulary instruction. |
| Templeton & Morris, 2001; Invernizzi & Hayes, 2004 | • Effective word study instruction reveals the historical structures inherent in English orthography. | • Sorts and lessons focus on the systematic progression of alphabet, pattern, and meaning. |
| Bear, D. R. & Helman, L., 2004; Bear, Templeton, Fashola, Drum, Mayer, & Kang, 1996; Helman & Baren, 2003; Helman, L. A., 2004; Weber & Longhi-Chirlin, 2001; Zutell & Allen, 1988 | • Students' first oral and written languages influence the way they learn to read and spell in English. Spelling errors among English language learners are predictable. | • *Words Their Way: Word Study in Action* highlights the specific needs of students at different points in their literacy development. Ways to tailor sorts to the language and developmental needs of students are provided for each sort and lesson. |

# Using Words Their Way In Your Literacy Block

*Words Their Way: Word Study in Action* can be used in conjunction with other reading, spelling, and vocabulary programs in your classroom. Introductory lessons may take about 20 minutes, but subsequent activities will last only about 10 to 15 minutes a day and do not require much teacher direction. Word study can fit easily into many parts of the day.

## Options for Using Words Their Way

*Words Their Way: Word Study in Action* can be used in a variety of classroom environments.

- **Guided reading:** If you use a guided reading program, *Words Their Way: Word Study in Action* is an excellent way to incorporate phonics into the curriculum.

- **Basal reading:** If you use a basal reading program, *Words Their Way: Word Study in Action* is an effective supplemental phonics resource that can be matched to the phonics skills you are teaching.

- **Stand-alone**: *Words Their Way: Word Study in Action* can also be used as a stand-alone spelling and phonics program.

## Getting Started

One of the benefits of the *Words Their Way: Word Study in Action* program is that all of the components you need for a week's worth of instruction are easily accessible. As you begin each week, mark the pages that correspond to the week's sort in your copy of the Word Study Notebook and in the Big Book of Rhymes. Set aside copies of the little book title from the *Words Their Way* Library you'll be using during the week, and print out the picture/word cards; game; Build, Blend, and Extend activity (if applicable); and any other materials you'll need. You may find it helpful to use file folders labeled with the different sort numbers to organize your instructional materials. A file folder is also ideal to use as a base for a game board; simply attach the two game board halves to an open file folder.

Decide where children will work. Space is needed for group work, individual work, and partner work. Separate areas on the floor or at tables in one part of the classroom to work with groups as they sort and discuss their results. Encourage other children to continue to work at their desk or in other areas of the room.

For more ideas about organizing word study in your classroom, see *Words Their Way: Word Study for Phonics, Vocabulary, and Spelling Instruction*, Chapter Three.

# How to Group Children

*Words Their Way: Word Study in Action* is designed to be used with small groups of five to ten children. Many teachers incorporate word study groups into small-group reading levels. Administering the Spell Check (found at the end of the Word Study Notebook) that corresponds to a specific skill strand can help you structure groups according to proficiency. Another easy way to group students is to determine whether they fall into the early, middle, or late stage of a particular level. The following chart highlights what you may see children use but confuse in their writing at different points in each *Words Their Way: Word Study in Action* level. Use the chart to help you decide where to place each child.

| | Early | Middle | Late |
|---|---|---|---|
| **Level K (On-level Grade K)** | • Drawing and scribbling for writing | • Letters, numbers, and letter-like forms<br>• Writing may wrap from right to left at the end of a line | • Substitutions of letters that sound, feel, and look alike: *Bp, Db* |
| **Level A (On-level Grade 1)** | • Letters based on point of articulation: J, JRF for *drive*<br>• Often long vowels by letter name | • Substitutions of letter name closest in point of articulation for short vowels<br>• Some consonant blends and digraphs | • Substitutions of common patterns for low frequency short vowels: COT for *caught* |
| **Level B (On-level Grade 2)** | • Long vowel markers: SNAIK for *snake*, FELE for *feel* | • Long vowel markers: NITE for *night*<br>• Consonant patterns: SMOCK for *smoke*<br>• Inventive substitutions in frequent, unstressed syllable patterns: TEACHAUR for *teacher*<br>• -ed and other common inflections: MARCHT for *marched*, BATID for *batted* | • Low frequency long vowel words: HIEGHT for *height*<br>• -ed and other common inflections<br>• Common Latin suffixes are spelled phonetically: ATTENSHUN for *attention* |
| **Level C (On-level Grade 3)** | • Consonant doubling: HOPING for *hopping*<br>• Long vowel patterns in accented syllable: PERAIDING or PERADDING for *parading*<br>• Reduced vowel in unaccented syllable: CIRCUL for *circle*<br>• Doubling and e drop: AMAZZING for *amazing* | • Some silent letters: EMFASIZE for *emphasize*, INDITEMENT for *indictment* | • Some suffixes and prefixes: ATTENSION for *attention*, PERTEND for *pretend*<br>• Vowel alternation in derivationally related pairs: COMPUSITION for *composition*<br>• Consonant alternations in derivationally related pairs: SPACIAL for *spatial* |

# Walk Through the Week

The lesson plan for each sort is presented in a logical and easy-to-follow way. It provides additional ideas for sorting, building vocabulary, helping English language learners, and using challenge words.

The **pictures and words** in the lesson are clearly identified.

Many lessons include additional **Challenge Words** that coordinate with the skills in the lesson for additional practice that is a bit more challenging.

**Objectives** identify the skill covered and describe what children accomplish in the lesson.

A list of **Materials** lets you see at a glance where to find each component used in the lesson.

---

 **Sort 8** — **Word Families  -op, -ot, -og**

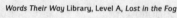

### Objectives

* To identify short *o* rhyming words
* To identify and sort pictures and words with *-op, -ot,* or *-og*

### Materials

 Big Book of Rhymes, Level A, "One Hot Day," page 15

 Teacher Resource CD, Level A

Word Study Notebook, Level A, pages 31–34

 *Words Their Way* Library, Level A, *Lost in the Fog*

Teacher Resource CD, Level A, Rock Hop Game

| Pictures/Words | | |
|---|---|---|
| *-op* | *-ot* | *-og* |
| mop | pot | frog |
| hop | dot | hog |
| top | hot | log |
| pop | cot | jog |

| **Challenge Words** | | |
|---|---|---|
| chop | slot | bog |
| plop | spot | cog |
| flop | plot | clog |
| shop | trot | |

---

## Day 1 — Introduce the Sort

In Levels K, A, and B, children listen as you read aloud a poem from the Big Book of Rhymes. They identify and discuss words in the poem that correspond to the lesson's skill. In the second half of the day's word-study session, you use the picture/word cards located on the Teacher Resource CD to model how to perform the week's sort.

### Day 1 — Introduce the Sort

*Whole Group*

 **Read a Rhyme: "One Hot Day"**

Introduce short *o* rhyming words by reading the poem "One Hot Day." As you read, emphasize the words that rhyme *(spot, hot; do, too).* As children find the rhyming words in the poem, write them in a column on the chalkboard or on chart paper. Help children understand that these words rhyme because they end with the same sound and letters. Read the poem again, omitting the last word of each line, and have children supply the missing word.

 **Introduce Picture/Word Sort -op, -ot, -og**

Print and cut apart the picture/word cards for Sort 8 from the Teacher Resource CD. Introduce the pictures and words, defining in context any words that are unfamiliar, such as *top, cot, hog,* and *jog.* Then demonstrate for children how to sort the pictures into -op, -ot, and -og word families. Ask children to describe how the pictures in each column are alike. *(They rhyme.)* Then introduce the word cards, and ask children to match each word card to its picture.

30

### Day 2 — Practice the Sort

*Whole Group/Independent*

 You may want to begin Days 2–5 by rereading the rhyme from Day 1. Then review the previous day's sort demonstration. Help children tear out page 31 from their Word Study Notebook and cut apart the cards.

Have children work independently or with a partner to sort the picture cards by ending sound, and then match the words and pictures in each word family. Have children say the names of the pictures and read the words as they work.

> **Alternative Sort: Identify My Category**
>
> When children are comfortable with this week's sort, re-sort the pictures or words into groups of living and nonliving things. Begin by sorting two or three of the pictures into the categories. When you pick up the next picture or word card, invite children to identify where it will go. Continue to do this until all the cards have been sorted and children are able to identify the categories.

---

## Day 2 — Practice the Sort

Review the sort with children and direct them to cut apart the picture/word cards in their Word Study Notebook. Children then sort their cards according to specific categories that reflect the sort skill.

An **Alternative Sort** provides another way for children to sort their picture/word cards.

## Day 3 — Find Words in Context

A corresponding book from the *Words Their Way* Library provides opportunities for both shared and independent reading, as children identify words from the text that reflect the target skill.

## Day 4 — Apply the Skill

Children demonstrate what they have learned by completing a writing activity found in the Word Study Notebook.

## Day 3 — Find Words in Context

*Whole Group/Independent/Partner*

Have children re-sort their cards. Then read *Lost in the Fog* with children. Have children listen for and identify any words that end with -op, -ot, or -og.

Have children look through their word cards to find words that match words in the text. Then have them read the story independently and find other words in the story that end with -op, -ot, or -og.

## Day 4 — Apply the Skill

*Independent/Partner*

Have children sort their cards again. Then have children turn to page 34 in their Word Study Notebook. Read aloud the directions, and encourage children work independently or with a partner to write words that end with -og, -ot, or -op.

## Day 5 — Complete the Sort

*Whole Group/Independent*

**Paste in Place**

Encourage children to sort and match their pictures and words into -op, -ot, and -og word families. Then have them turn to page 33 in their Word Study Notebook and paste the pictures and matching words in the correct column for each word family.

**Play the Game**

When children are finished, they may play the Rock Hop game. (See the Teacher Resource CD for the game board, playing cards, and directions.)

---

**Building Vocabulary**

If children are unfamiliar with the word *jog*, explain that it means "to run at a slow, steady pace." Invite children to stand up and practice jogging in place.

**ESL/ELL English Language Learners**

Review the pictures and words with children. You may need to explain that a *hog* is similar to a *pig*, that a *cot* is a small bed, and that *jog* is the same as *run*. Have children pronounce each word to be sure they are differentiating among the three endings -op, -ot, and -og.

**Challenge Words Activity**

Ask children to find other words that end with -op, -ot, or -og. (If children need prompting, make suggestions from the Challenge Words list on the facing page.) Then have children make word cards for these new words. They can work in small groups to sort the words into categories.

**Teacher Tip**

During a second or repeated sort, do not correct children when they place a picture or word in the wrong column. Wait until they have completed the sort, and have them read the words in each column to check them. If they still don't find the misplaced picture or word, tell them which column it is in, and have them find it.

You may wish to use the Sort 8 **Build, Blend, and Extend**. (See the Teacher Resource CD.)

31

**Building Vocabulary** provides meanings for unfamiliar words and pictures and suggests a strategy to help children understand words they don't know.

**English Language Learners** presents extra support for children through additional exploration of vocabulary in context, unfamiliar blends and vowel sounds, and other concepts that English language learners may find difficult.

**Challenge Words Activity** provides a sorting activity that can be used with the Challenge Words listed on the previous page.

**Teacher Tip** gives a suggestion designed to aid in areas such as instruction, assessment, and classroom management.

## Day 5 — Complete the Sort

Children sort their cards one final time and paste them into place on the grid in the Word Study Notebook. In the second half of the day's word study session, children play a game found on the Teacher Resource CD, such as Bingo! or Go Fish, that helps them apply the skills in the sort.

17

# Meeting Individual Differences

Recognizing not only a child's spelling stage, but also his or her level within the stage, will help you know when to teach what. Children in Grade 1, for example, may be in the early, middle, or late level of the Letter Name-Alphabetic stage, or they may be in the late level of the previous stage (Emergent) or the early level of the next stage (Within Word Pattern).

To address this issue, sorts for the second half of the previous level and the first half of the next level are included (when applicable) on a specific level's Teacher Resource CD, ensuring that *Words Their Way: Word Study in Action* provides flexibility for all the varied instructional levels in your classroom.

In addition, you may find that your students can move through the sorts very quickly. In that case, you may wish to use more than one complete level kit in your classroom.

**English language learners** Each lesson plan in *Words Their Way: Word Study in Action* provides a suggestion for adapting the lesson to better fit the needs of English language learners. The tips cover a range of concepts that English language learners may find difficult, including letters and sounds that may be different from those in their native language, unusual spelling patterns, and vocabulary in context.

**Family involvement** The inside front cover of the Word Study Notebook provides an at-home activity for families to do with their children each night from Monday through Thursday.

# Progress Monitoring and Using the Spell Checks

To monitor children's word study progress, you can include a combination of writing samples, observations during oral reading, and analysis of spelling errors in formal assessments. The Spell Checks provided in each level of *Words Their Way: Word Study in Action* are another valuable assessment tool. Spell Checks are provided in the back of the Word Study Notebook. They can be used as pretests to help determine how children should be grouped, or to assess whether children need to do the sorts in a specific skill strand. Then, as children complete each series of skills, administer the corresponding Spell Check to determine what they have learned and what they do not understand. Use the results of the Spell Check to plan for individual or small-group instruction.

**Spell Check 1: Rhyming Words** Use this Spell Check after completing Sort 7. This Spell Check assesses children's ability to identify rhyming sounds. If children miss rhyming words in a specific word family, have them review the sort for that word family. If children miss an unusually high number of rhyming words, they should not proceed to the next sort until they have reviewed the previous sorts.

**Spell Check 2: Letter Recognition** Use this Spell Check after completing Sort 16. This Spell Check assesses children's ability to write matching capital and lowercase letters. Watch for these types of errors: If children write *p* with *B*, review Sorts 8 and 13; if children write *b* with *D*, review Sorts 8 and 10.

**Spell Check 3: Beginning Sounds** Use this Spell Check after completing Sort 26 with children. This Spell Check assesses children's ability to identify initial consonant sounds. If children miss a beginning consonant, have them review the corresponding sort for that letter. If children miss an unusually high number of beginning consonants, they should not proceed to the next sort until they have reviewed the previous sorts.

**Spell Check 4: Word Families** Use this Spell Check after completing Sort 32 with children. This Spell Check assesses children's ability to spell and write the ending letters in one-syllable short vowel words. Watch for these types of errors: If you see a pattern of writing *-an* for *-en*, review Sort 32 with children; if children write *-en* for *-in*, review Sorts 28, 30, and 32.

**Spell Check 5: Short Vowel Sounds** Use this Spell Check after completing Sort 36 with children. This Spell Check assesses children's ability to distinguish among short vowels and recognize short vowel words. If children consistently choose words from the wrong vowel family, have them review the corresponding sorts for those families.

# Concept Sort Shapes

## Objectives

- To explore the concept of sorting
- To identify and sort circles, squares, and triangles

## Materials

 Big Book of Rhymes, Level K, "I See Shapes," page 5

 Teacher Resource CD, Level K, Sort 1

 Word Study Notebook, Level K, pages 3–6

 *Words Their Way* Library, Level K, *Six Go By*

 Teacher Resource CD, Level K, Sort Ourselves game

### Pictures

| circles | squares |
|---|---|
| red circle | yellow square |
| yellow circle | blue square |
| blue circle | red square |
| blue circle | red square |

*triangles*
red triangle
blue triangle
yellow triangle
yellow triangle

---

## Day 1 — Introduce the Sort

*Whole Group*

 **Read a Rhyme: "I See Shapes"**

Read aloud "I See Shapes" several times until children become familiar with the rhyme. Track the text as you read by pointing to each word. Next, read and track the first and second lines of the rhyme until children have memorized them. Call on volunteers to track these lines as you and the group read them aloud. When children have demonstrated that they can track accurately, encourage several volunteers to track specific words such as *see* and *one*. Finally, have children search the poem and illustration for word and picture examples of *circles, squares,* and *triangles.*

 **Introduce Picture Sort *Shapes***

Print out and cut apart the picture cards for Sort 1 from the Teacher Resource CD. Display the cards one at a time, and ask children to name each shape. Then demonstrate for children how to sort the cards according to shape (triangle, circle, square). Ask children how the pictures in each column are alike and how they are different. *(They are the same shape; they are different sizes.)*

## Day 2 — Practice the Sort

*Whole Group/Partner/Independent*

 You may want to begin Days 2–5 by rereading the rhyme from Day 1. Then review the previous day's sort. Help children tear out page 3 from their Word Study Notebook and cut apart the cards.

Have children work independently or with a partner to say the name of each shape (circle, square, triangle) and, using the grid on page 5 of their Word Study Notebook, sort their cards according to shape.

### Alternative Sort: Color Sort

When children are comfortable sorting by shape, have them work independently or with a partner to re-sort the cards according to color (red, blue, yellow). Remind children that the pictures in each group will be different kinds of shapes but the same color.

## Day 3 — Find Words in Context

*Whole Group*

Have children re-sort their cards. Then read *Six Go By* with children. Then leaf through the pages, discussing the illustrations. Ask children to be "shape detectives " by pointing out and naming the three shapes in this week's sort (circle, square, and triangle).

## Day 4 — Apply the Skill

*Independent/Partner*

Have children sort their cards again. Then have them turn to page 6 in their Word Study Notebook. Read aloud the directions, and have children work independently or with a partner to draw triangles, circles, and squares in the correct columns.

## Day 5 — Complete the Sort

*Whole Group/Independent*

### Paste in Place

Have children turn to page 5 in their Word Study Notebook. Point out the shapes at the top of the grid, and review how to sort the cards according to shape. Encourage children to say the name of each picture as they sort the cards. Then have children paste the picture cards in place on the page.

### Play the Game

When children are finished, they may play Sort Ourselves. (See the Teacher Resource CD for playing directions.)

---

### ESL/ELL  English Language Learners

Ahead of time, gather items to represent the shapes on the cards (for example, a circular roll of tape, a drafting triangle, and square sticky notes). Review the picture cards, naming the shapes. Then work with children to name the shapes of the items you have collected.

### Teacher Tip

Triangles may confuse children, since their appearance can differ depending on the size of the angles. Explain that any shape with three sides and three corners is a triangle.

## Sort 2

# Concept Sort Food, Clothes, Toys

## Objectives

- To explore the concept of sorting
- To identify and sort food, clothes, and toys

## Materials

 Big Book of Rhymes, Level K, "Lunch at the Beach," page 7

 Teacher Resource CD, Level K, Sort 2

 Word Study Notebook, Level K, pages 7–10

 *Words Their Way* Library, Level K, *School Lunch*

 Teacher Resource CD, Level K, Guess the Category game

### Pictures

| *food* | *clothes* |
|--------|-----------|
| corn | shirt |
| celery | coat |
| apple | cap |
| cheese | sock |

*toys*
blocks
ball
jump rope
stuffed toy

---

## Day 1 Introduce the Sort

*Whole Group*

### Read a Rhyme: "Lunch at the Beach"

Read aloud "Lunch at the Beach" several times until children become familiar with the rhyme. Track the text as you read by pointing to each word. Next, read and track the first and second lines of the rhyme until children have memorized them. Call on volunteers to track these lines as you and the group read them aloud. When children have demonstrated that they can track accurately, encourage several volunteers to track specific words such as *pack* and *lunch*. Finally, have children search the poem for words that name foods, clothes, and toys.

### Introduce Picture Sort
*Food, Clothes, Toys*

Print out and cut apart the cards for Sort 2 from the Teacher Resource CD. Introduce the pictures, identifying any that are unfamiliar. Demonstrate how to sort the pictures into three categories: food, clothes, and toys. Ask a volunteer to name his or her favorite food and point out the column in which a picture of that food would appear. Continue with similar questions.

## Day 2 Practice the Sort

*Whole Group/Partner/Independent*

You may want to begin Days 2–5 by rereading the rhyme from Day 1. Then review the previous day's sort. Help children tear out page 7 from their Word Study Notebook and cut apart the cards.

Have children work independently or with a partner to name each item. Then, using the grid on page 9 of their Word Study Notebook, have them sort their cards according to whether the picture shows food, clothing, or a toy.

---

**Alternative Sort:
Bigger Than a Milk Carton**

When children are comfortable with this week's sort, have them re-sort their pictures according to size. Show children a ring and an empty 1-quart milk carton. Ask children if they think the ring will fit into the carton. *(yes)* Confirm the answer by dropping the ring into the carton. Ask if a large book would fit. *(no)* Finally, have children sort their cards into two piles: things that would fit in the carton and things that would not.

22

## Day 3
## Find Words in Context

*Whole Group*

Have children re-sort their cards. Then show children the cover of *School Lunch*. Discuss ways the illustration resembles the lunch line at your school. (If children do not eat lunch at school, you may need to explain school lunch procedures.) Ask children to listen closely to find out what food is being served. Then ask volunteers to name the foods as you read aloud the book.

## Day 4
## Apply the Skill

*Independent/Partner*

Have children sort their cards again. Then have them turn to page 10 in their Word Study Notebook. Read aloud the directions, and encourage children to work independently or with a partner to draw different kinds of food, clothes, and toys.

## Day 5
## Complete the Sort

*Whole Group/Independent*

### Paste in Place

Have children turn to page 9 in their Word Study Notebook. Encourage them to sort their cards according to whether they are food, clothes, or toys, naming each picture as they work. Then have them paste the pictures in place on the page.

### Play the Game

When children are finished, they may play Guess the Category. (See the Teacher Resource CD for game materials and playing directions.)

**ESL/ELL** ## English Language Learners

Review the cards with children, naming each picture. Then use the picture names in a game of Simon Says. For example, touch your sock and say, "Simon says, 'Touch your sock,'" or pretend to bounce a ball as you say, "Simon says, 'Bounce a ball.'" Remind children to copy your action only if you say, "Simon says" before the command.

## Teacher Tip

Throughout the year, help children take advantage of other opportunities to practice sorting. For example, as part of a science lesson, children can sort leaves or rocks according to size, shape, or color.

# Rhyming Sort -at, -an

## Objectives

- To identify short *a* rhyming words
- To sort pictures that rhyme with *-at* and *-an*

## Materials

Big Book of Rhymes, Level K, "The Man, the Cat, and the Hat," page 9

Teacher Resource CD, Level K, Sort 3

Word Study Notebook, Level K, pages 11–14

*Words Their Way* Library, Level K, *Fat Cat*

Teacher Resource CD, Level K, Bingo! game

### Pictures

| -at | -an |
|-----|-----|
| pat | can |
| hat | fan |
| bat | Dan |
| mat | van |
| rat | man |
| cat | Nan |

### Challenge Words

| | |
|------|------|
| sat | ban |
| fat | tan |
| brat | plan |
| chat | scan |
| flat | |
| that | |

## Day 1 — Introduce the Sort

*Whole Group*

### Read a Rhyme: "The Man, the Cat, and the Hat"

Read aloud "The Man, the Cat, and the Hat" several times until children become familiar with the rhyme. Track the text as you read by pointing to each word. Next, read and track the first and second lines of the rhyme until children have memorized them. Call on volunteers to track these lines as you and the group read them aloud. When children have demonstrated that they can track accurately, encourage several volunteers to track specific words such as *hat* and *Pat*. Finally, have children search the poem for words that rhyme with *cat* and *man*.

### Introduce Picture Sort -at, -an

Print out and cut apart the cards for Sort 3. Introduce the pictures, identifying *Nan, Dan, pat,* and any others that might be unfamiliar. Then demonstrate how to sort the pictures according to whether their names rhyme with *cat* or *pan*. Lead children in naming the pictures and describing how the names are alike.

## Day 2 — Practice the Sort

*Whole Group/Partner/Independent*

You may want to begin Days 2–5 by rereading the rhyme from Day 1. Then review the previous day's sort. Help children tear out page 11 from their Word Study Notebook and cut apart the cards.

Have children work independently or with a partner to say the name of each picture. Then, using the grid on page 13 of their Word Study Notebook, have children sort their picture cards into two groups: names that rhyme with *cat* and names that rhyme with *pan*.

> **Alternative Sort: Memory Check**
>
> When children have completed this week's sort, ask them to recall the poem, "The Man, the Cat, and the Hat." If needed, review what happens in the poem. Then ask children to sort the cards into two piles: one with items found in the poem and one with other items.

## Day 3 Find Words in Context

*Whole Group*

Have children re-sort their cards. Then read *Fat Cat* with children. Ask children to listen for and identify words that rhyme with *fat*. *(bat, sat, rat, cat)* Ask questions about the story that can be answered with -*at* words, such as, "What animal sits on the branch first?" *(bat)*

## Day 4 Apply the Skill

*Independent/Partner*

Have children sort their cards again. Then have them turn to page 14 in their Word Study Notebook. Read aloud the directions, and encourage children to work independently or with a partner to draw pictures of things whose names rhyme with *cat* and *pan*.

## Day 5 Complete the Sort

*Whole Group/Independent*

### Paste in Place

Have children turn to page 13 in their Word Study Notebook. Encourage children to say the name of each picture and sort their pictures into two categories: names that rhyme with *cat* and names that rhyme with *pan*. Then have them paste the pictures in place on the page.

### Play the Game

When children are finished, they may play Bingo! (See the Teacher Resource CD for game materials and playing directions.)

## Building Vocabulary

Children may assume that the picture cards for *Nan* and *Dan* represent words such as *person* or *child*. Explain to children that *Dan* and *Nan* are the names of the specific children in the pictures. Point out that *Dan* and *Nan* rhyme with the other -*an* words in the sort, while *person* and *child* do not. Children may also have trouble identifying the picture card for *pat*, since the picture shows an action rather than an item. Help them conceptualize the word by patting different objects in the classroom and then encouraging them to pat specific items (their desks, books, etc.).

## ESL/ELL English Language Learners

Review the cards with children, naming each picture. Then help children practice the plural form of the words by asking volunteers to complete sentences such as "I saw one cat, but Tang saw two [cats]." Be sure to explain that *men* is the irregular plural for *man*.

## Challenge Words Activity

Challenge children to think of other words that rhyme with *cat* and *pan* and are not pictured in the sort. (Refer to the Challenge Words list on the facing page, if necessary.)

## Teacher Tip

Consider establishing a "reading chair," where children gather when you read to them. As children learn to associate the chair with reading, they will automatically prepare to listen to a story or poem when they gather at that location.

# Rhyming Sort  -ad, -ap, -ag

## Objectives

- To identify short *a* rhyming words
- To sort pictures that rhyme with *-ad*, *-ap*, and *-ag*

## Materials

 Big Book of Rhymes, Level K, "The Best Cap," page 11

 Teacher Resource CD, Level K, Sort 4

 Word Study Notebook, Level K, pages 15–18

  *Words Their Way* Library, Level K, *Caps*

 Teacher Resource CD, Level K, Concentration game

### Pictures

| -ad | -ap | -ag |
|-----|-----|-----|
| mad | lap | sag |
| pad | nap | wag |
| lad | rap | bag |
| dad | cap | rag |

### Challenge Words

| | | |
|-----|-----|-----|
| bad | gap | nag |
| had | tap | brag |
| glad | snap | drag |
| | clap | snag |

---

## Day 1 Introduce the Sort

*Whole Group*

 **Read a Rhyme: "The Best Cap"**

Read aloud "The Best Cap" several times until children become familiar with the rhyme. Track the text as you read by pointing to each word. Next, read and track the third and fourth lines of the rhyme until children have memorized them. Call on volunteers to track these lines as you and the group read them aloud. When children have demonstrated that they can track accurately, encourage several volunteers to track specific words such as *cap* and *best*. Finally, have children search the poem for words that rhyme with *sad*, *map*, and *tag*.

 **Introduce Picture Sort -ad, -ap, -ag**

Print out and cut apart the cards for Sort 4. Introduce the pictures, identifying *rap*, *lad*, and any others that may be unfamiliar. Then demonstrate how to sort the pictures according to whether their names rhyme with *sad*, *map*, or *tag*. Lead children in naming the pictures in each column, and ask them to describe how the names are alike.

## Day 2 Practice the Sort

*Whole Group/Partner/Independent*

 You may want to begin Days 2–5 by rereading the rhyme from Day 1. Then review the previous day's picture sort. Help children tear out page 15 from their Word Study Notebook and cut apart the cards.

Have children work independently or with a partner to say the name of each picture. Then, using the grid on page 17 of their Word Study Notebook, have children sort their picture cards into three groups: names that rhyme with *sad*, names that rhyme with *map*, and names that rhyme with *tag*.

> **Alternate Sort: Fold It!**
>
> When children have completed this week's sort, have them work independently or with a partner to re-sort the picture cards into two categories: things that can be folded in half and things that cannot be folded. When they have completed the sort, ask children to explain their reasoning.

**Day 3**

## Find Words in Context

*Whole Group*

Have children re-sort their cards. Then read *Caps* with children. Ask them to listen for and identify any words that rhyme with *cap*. *(flap, nap)* Ask if all the caps in the story are the same. *(no)* Discuss the concept that although the caps differ, they are all caps and therefore all belong in the same group or category.

**Day 4**

## Apply the Skill

*Independent/Partner*

Have children sort their cards again. Then have them turn to page 18 in their Word Study Notebook. Read aloud the directions, and encourage children to work independently or with a partner to draw pictures of things whose names rhyme with *sad, map,* and *tag.*

**Day 5**

## Complete the Sort

*Whole Group/Independent*

### Paste in Place

Have children turn to page 17 of their Word Study Notebook. Encourage children to say the name of each picture and sort their pictures into three categories: names that rhyme with *sad,* names that rhyme with *map,* and names that rhyme with *tag.* Then have them paste the pictures in place on the page.

### Play the Game

When children are finished, they may play Concentration. (See the Teacher Resource CD for game materials and playing directions.)

## Building Vocabulary

Explain to children that *lad* is another word for "boy" or "young man." Discuss how the picture card for the word helps children conceptualize its meaning.

## English Language Learners

Review the cards with children, naming each picture. You may need to explain that *rap* means "to knock," *wag* means "to move something back and forth" (a finger or tail, for example), and *nap* means "to sleep for a short time." Invite volunteers to act out these three words, and ask children to share words with similar meanings in their native language.

## Challenge Words Activity

Challenge children to think of other words that rhyme with *sad, map,* or *tag* and are not pictured in the sort. (Refer to the Challenge Words list on the facing page, if necessary.)

## Teacher Tip

Try using hand movements to capture children's attention as you read the rhyme on Day 1. For example, pat your head as you read the words *on my head,* or cradle your head in your hands when you read the words *take a nap.* Invite children to imitate the movements as you read.

# Rhyming Sort -op, -ot, -og

## Objectives

- To identify short *o* rhyming words
- To sort pictures that rhyme with *-op*, *-ot*, and *-og*

## Materials

 Big Book of Rhymes, Level K, "More Popcorn, Please," page 13

 Teacher Resource CD, Level K, Sort 5

 Word Study Notebook, Level K, pages 19–22

 *Words Their Way* Library, Level K, *Popcorn*

 Teacher Resource CD, Level K, Bingo! game

### Pictures

| -op | -ot | -og |
|------|------|------|
| shop | pot | frog |
| hop | dot | log |
| top | cot | hog |
| mop | hot | fog |

### Challenge Words

| | | |
|------|------|------|
| pop | got | bog |
| chop | lot | cog |
| crop | not | clog |
| drop | spot | |

---

## Day 1 — Introduce the Sort

*Whole Group*

### Read a Rhyme: "More Popcorn, Please"

Read aloud "More Popcorn, Please" several times until children become familiar with the rhyme. Track the text as you read by pointing to each word. Next, read and track the fifth and sixth lines of the rhyme until children have memorized them. Call on volunteers to track these lines as you and the group read them aloud. When children have demonstrated that they can track accurately, encourage several volunteers to track specific words such as *like* and *feed*. Finally, have children search the poem for words that rhyme with *top, pot,* and *dog.*

### Introduce Picture Sort *-op, -ot, -og*

Print out and cut apart the cards for Sort 5. Introduce the pictures, identifying *fog, cot,* and any others that might be unfamiliar. Then demonstrate how to sort the pictures according to whether their names rhyme with *top, pot,* or *dog.* Lead children in naming the pictures in each column, and ask them to describe how the names are alike.

## Day 2 — Practice the Sort

*Whole Group/Partner/Independent*

You may want to begin Days 2–5 by rereading the rhyme from Day 1. Then review the previous day's sort. Help children tear out page 19 from their Word Study Notebook and cut apart the cards.

Have children work independently or with a partner to name each picture. Then, using the grid on page 21 of their Word Study Notebook, have children sort their cards into three groups: names that rhyme with *top*, names that rhyme with *pot*, and names that rhyme with *dog*.

### Alternative Sort: School Supplies

When children have completed this week's sort, have them work independently or with a partner to re-sort the picture cards into two categories: things that can be found in your school and things that cannot. Remind children that in addition to classrooms, the school includes areas such as the lunchroom, the janitor's supply room, and the nurse's office.

## Day 3 Find Words in Context

*Whole Group*

Have children re-sort their cards. Then as you read *Popcorn*, have children listen for and name words that rhyme with *pop*. *(top, stop)* Then reread the book and tell children to "pop up like popcorn" (hop up and then sit down quickly) each time they hear a word that ends like *pop*. Read aloud slowly, allowing time for children to "pop." Finally, review story words with the *-ot* sound. *(pot, hot)*

## Day 4 Apply the Skill

*Independent/Partner*

Have children sort their cards again. Then have them turn to page 22 in their Word Study Notebook. Read aloud the directions, and have children work independently or with a partner to draw pictures of things whose names rhyme with *top, pot,* and *dog.*

## Day 5 Complete the Sort

*Whole Group/Independent*

### Paste in Place

Have children turn to page 21 in their Word Study Notebook. Encourage children to say the name of each picture and sort their pictures into three categories: words that rhyme with *top*, words that rhyme with *pot*, and words that rhyme with *dog*. Then have them paste the pictures in place on the page.

### Play the Game

When children are finished, they may play Bingo! (See the Teacher Resource CD for game materials and playing directions.)

## Building Vocabulary

Identify the *fog* picture card for children, and explain that fog is made up of very tiny drops of water in the air. Discuss the concept of fog by asking children what they know about fog: what it looks and feels like, where you might see fog, when it might be foggy, and so on.

## ESL/ELL English Language Learners

Review the cards with children, naming each picture. To practice vocabulary and pronunciation, show the picture of the pot and the picture of the cot, and ask which would be used for cooking. *(pot)* Continue with other pictures and similar questions.

## Challenge Words Activity

Challenge children to think of other words that rhyme with *top, pot,* or *dog* and are not pictured in the sort. (Refer to the Challenge Words list on the facing page, if necessary.)

## Teacher Tip

When asking children questions, allow ample wait time before calling on a child. This accommodates children who need extra time to consider a question and formulate a response.

# Rhyming Sort -et, -eg, -en

## Objectives

- To identify short *e* rhyming words
- To sort pictures that rhyme with *-et*, *-eg*, and *-en*

## Materials

**Big Book of Rhymes, Level K, "Greg and Peg," page 15**

Teacher Resource CD, Level K, Sort 6

Word Study Notebook, Level K, pages 23–26

*Words Their Way* Library, Level K, *Going Fishing*

Teacher Resource CD, Level K, Concentration game

### Pictures

| -et | -eg | -en |
|-----|-----|-----|
| pet | beg | hen |
| net | leg | men |
| vet | Meg | pen |
| wet | peg | ten |

### Challenge Words

| bet | Greg | den |
|-----|------|------|
| get | | when |
| let | | then |
| met | | |

---

## Day 1 Introduce the Sort

*Whole Group*

### Read a Rhyme: "Greg and Peg"

Read aloud "Greg and Peg" several times until children become familiar with the rhyme. Track the text as you read by pointing to each word. Next, read and track the fifth and sixth lines of the rhyme until children have memorized them. Call on volunteers to track these lines as you and the group read them aloud. When children have demonstrated that they can track accurately, encourage several volunteers to track specific words such as *said* and *feed*. Finally, have children search the poem for words that rhyme with *jet, leg,* and *pen*.

### Introduce Picture Sort -et, -eg, -en

Print out and cut apart the cards for Sort 6. Introduce the pictures, identifying *Meg, vet, wet,* and any others that might be unfamiliar. Then demonstrate how to sort the pictures according to whether their names rhyme with *jet, leg,* or *pen*. Have children name the pictures in each column and tell how the picture names are alike. *(They rhyme.)*

## Day 2 Practice the Sort

*Whole Group/Partner/Independent*

You may want to begin Days 2–5 by rereading the rhyme from Day 1. Then review the previous day's sort. Help children tear out page 23 from their Word Study Notebook and cut apart the cards.

Have children work independently or with a partner to name each picture. Then, using the grid on page 25 of their Word Study Notebook, have them sort their cards into three groups: names that rhyme with *jet*, names that rhyme with *leg*, and names that rhyme with *pen*.

### Alternative Sort: Stump the Teacher

Without looking at the pictures, distribute a picture card from the sort to each child. Explain that children will be giving you clues about their picture. You will get one chance to guess the identity of each picture. Depending upon your answer, the child should place the card in a pile for correct guesses or a pile for incorrect guesses. Repeat the routine with other children.

## Day 3 — Find Words in Context

*Whole Group*

Have children re-sort their cards. Then show children the cover of *Going Fishing*, and explain that the man in the illustration is getting ready for a fishing trip. Read the book to find out what he takes along. Stop after each page to allow children to name the things the man takes and to identify words that end in the -*et* sound. *(net, pet, jet)*

## Day 4 — Apply the Skill

*Independent/Partner*

Have children sort their cards again. Then have them turn to page 26 in their Word Study Notebook. Read aloud the directions, and encourage children to work independently or with a partner to draw pictures of things whose names rhyme with *jet*, *leg*, and *pen*.

## Day 5 — Complete the Sort

*Whole Group/Independent*

### Paste in Place

Have children turn to page 25 in their Word Study Notebook. Encourage children to say the name of each picture and sort their pictures into three categories: words that rhyme with *jet*, words that rhyme with *leg*, and words that rhyme with *pen*. Then have them paste the pictures in place on the page.

### Play the Game

When children are finished, they may play Concentration. (See the Teacher Resource CD for game materials and playing directions.)

## Building Vocabulary

Children may assume that the *jet* picture in the grid on page 25 represents the word *airplane* or *plane*. Explain that a jet is a type of airplane that uses a certain kind of engine.

## ESL/ELL English Language Learners

Review the cards with children. Name each picture, and have children repeat the picture name after you. Model each word in a sentence to help children understand the word's meaning. Make sure children are differentiating among the three rhyming endings -*et*, -*eg*, and -*en*.

## Challenge Words Activity

Challenge children to think of other words that rhyme with *jet*, *leg*, or *pen* and are not pictured in the sort. (Refer to the Challenge Words list on the facing page, if necessary.)

## Teacher Tip

Encourage children to develop their sorting prowess by participating in basic sorting exercises that identify common objects (pencils, buttons, colors, and so on) in the classroom.

# Rhyming Sort -ug, -ut, -un

## Objectives

- To identify short *u* rhyming words
- To sort pictures that rhyme with *-ug*, *-ut*, and *-un*

## Materials

 Big Book of Rhymes, Level K, "Keep Out!," page 17

 Teacher Resource CD, Level K, Sort 7

 Word Study Notebook, Level K, pages 27–30

 *Words Their Way* Library, Level K, *Little Bug*

 Teacher Resource CD, Level K, Go Fish game

### Pictures

| -ug | -ut | -un |
|-----|-----|-----|
| jug | nut | fun |
| rug | cut | run |
| tug | rut | bun |
| mug | shut | sun |

### Challenge Words

| | | |
|-----|-----|-----|
| dug | gut | pun |
| hug | jut | stun |
| lug | strut | spun |
| slug | | |

---

## Introduce the Sort

*Whole Group*

 **Read a Rhyme: "Keep Out!"**

Read aloud "Keep Out!" several times until children become familiar with the rhyme. Track the text as you read by pointing to each word. Next, read and track the first and second lines of the rhyme until children have memorized them. Call on volunteers to track these lines as you and the group read them aloud. When children have demonstrated that they can track accurately, encourage several volunteers to track specific words such as *bug* and *in*. Finally, have children search the poem for words that rhyme with *bug*, *hut*, and *bun*.

 **Introduce Picture Sort -ug, -ut, -un**

Print out and cut apart the cards for Sort 7 from the Teacher Resource CD. Introduce the pictures, identifying *rut, tug*, and any others that are unfamiliar. Then demonstrate how to sort the pictures according to whether their names rhyme with *bug, hut,* or *bun*. Point to each card and ask children to name the picture, encouraging them to listen for the rhyme.

## Practice the Sort

*Whole Group/Partner/Independent*

 You may want to begin Days 2–5 by rereading the rhyme from Day 1. Then review the previous day's sort. Help children tear out page 27 from their Word Study Notebook and cut apart the cards.

Have children work independently or with a partner to name each picture. Then, using the grid on page 29 of their Word Study Notebook, have children sort their cards into three groups: names that rhyme with *bug*, names that rhyme with *hut*, and names that rhyme with *bun*.

### Alternative Sort: Action!

When children are comfortable with this week's sort, suggest that they re-sort their pictures according to type of word. Explain that some words (verbs) are action words. Together, brainstorm some action words, such as *read, play,* and *jump*. Then have children sort their pictures into two columns, action words and other words.

**Day 3**

## Find Words in Context

*Whole Group*

Have children re-sort their cards. Then read *Little Bug* with children. Ask them to listen for words that rhyme with *bug*. Tell children there are six words that rhyme with *bug* in the book. Challenge children to recall all six words. *(mug, plug, rug, jug, tug, hug)* If they have trouble recalling the words, reread the book, allowing children to stop you when you reach a word that rhymes with *bug*.

**Day 4**

## Apply the Skill

*Independent/Partner*

Have children sort their cards again. Then have them turn to page 30 in their Word Study Notebook. Read aloud the directions, and encourage children to work independently or with a partner to draw pictures of things whose names rhyme with *bug, hut,* and *bun.*

**Day 5**

## Complete the Sort

*Whole Group/Independent*

### Paste in Place

Have children turn to page 29 in their Word Study Notebook. Encourage children to say the name of each picture and sort their pictures into three categories: words that rhyme with *bug*, words that rhyme with *hut*, and words that rhyme with *bun*. Then have them paste the pictures in place on the page.

### Play the Game

When children are finished, they may play Go Fish. (See the Teacher Resource CD for playing cards and directions.)

## Building Vocabulary

If children are unfamiliar with the word *rut*, explain that it is a groove in the ground that is usually made by the wheels of cars, trains, or other vehicles.

## ESL/ELL English Language Learners

If possible, bring the following containers to class: mug, teacup, pitcher, jug. Set the mug and cup side by side, and discuss the differences in shape and size. Similarly, discuss how a jug is different from a pitcher.

## Challenge Words Activity

Challenge children to think of other words that rhyme with *bug, hut,* or *bun* and are not pictured in the sort. (Refer to the Challenge Words list on the facing page, if necessary.)

## Teacher Tip

When possible, reinforce learning by referring back to various pictures and rhyming sounds throughout the day. For example, when children are recording weather conditions on the class calendar, take a minute to review the word *sun* and brainstorm words that rhyme with it.

 **Spell Check 1**

After completing Sorts 1–7, you may want to administer Spell Check 1 in the Word Study Notebook on page 147. See page 19 for instructions on progress monitoring and using the Spell Check.

# Letter Recognition  Aa, Bb, Tt

## Objectives

- To recognize the letters *Aa*, *Bb*, and *Tt*
- To identify and sort different print styles and cases of *Aa*, *Bb*, and *Tt*

## Materials

 Big Book of Rhymes, Level K, "Billy's Toy Box," page 19

 Teacher Resource CD, Level K, Sort 8

 Word Study Notebook, Level K, pages 31–34

 *Words Their Way* Library, Level K, *The Toy Box*

 Teacher Resource CD, Level K, Find the Letter game

### Letters

| Aa | Bb |
|---|---|
| 4 variations of *A* | 4 variations of *B* |
| 4 variations of *a* | 4 variations of *b* |

**Tt**

4 variations of *T*

4 variations of *t*

---

## Day 1  Introduce the Sort

*Whole Group*

 **Read a Rhyme: "Billy's Toy Box"**

Read aloud "Billy's Toy Box" several times until children become familiar with the rhyme. Track the text as you read by pointing to each word. Next, read and track the third and fourth lines of the rhyme until children have memorized them. Call on volunteers to track these lines as you and the group read them aloud. When children have demonstrated that they can track accurately, encourage several volunteers to track specific words such as *toy* and *takes*. Finally, have children search the poem to find examples of capital and lowercase *Aa*, *Bb*, and *Tt*.

 **Introduce Letter Sort *Aa*, *Bb*, *Tt***

Print out and cut apart the cards for Sort 8. Show the cards and ask children to name each letter after you. Then demonstrate how to sort the cards by letter names *Aa*, *Bb*, and *Tt*. Select two lowercase *t* cards, and ask children how the letters are different. Select a capital and lowercase *t*, and ask how they differ. Remind children that despite the differences, the letters are all named *t*. Continue with *a* and *b*.

## Day 2  Practice the Sort

*Whole Group/Partner/Independent*

 You may want to begin Days 2–5 by rereading the rhyme from Day 1. Then review the previous day's sort. Help children tear out page 31 from their Word Study Notebook and cut apart the letter cards.

Have children work independently or with a partner to say the name of each letter and, using the grid on page 33 in their Word Study Notebook, sort the cards by letter names.

**Alternative Sort: Case Study**

When children are comfortable with this week's sort, re-sort the letters into capital and lowercase categories. Begin by sorting three or four of the cards. When you pick up the next letter card, invite children to guess where it will go. Continue until all the cards have been sorted.

**Day 3**

## Find Words in Context

*Whole Group*

Have children re-sort their cards. Then read aloud *The Toy Box* with children. Direct their attention to the cover of the book, and have them look in the title for the capital letters *T* and *B*. Continue page by page as children identify capital and lowercase *a*, *b*, and *t*.

**Day 4**

## Apply the Skill

*Whole Group/Independent*

Have children sort their cards again. Then have them turn to page 34 in their Word Study Notebook. Read aloud the directions, and guide children in printing the first few letters in the activity. Have children say the name of each letter aloud before they print it. If necessary, demonstrate how to form the letters.

**Day 5**

## Complete the Sort

*Whole Group/Independent*

### Paste in Place

Have children turn to page 33 in their Word Study Notebook. Ask them to say the name of each letter at the top of the grid. Then have them sort their cards by letter name and paste the cards into the correct column for each letter.

### Play the Game

When children are finished, they may play Find the Letter. (See the Teacher Resource CD for game materials and playing directions.)

**ESL/ELL English Language Learners**

Review the cards with children, naming each letter. Have children say the letter names after you. Show a T-shirt to children, spreading it out on the table or floor. Ask children to guess how the shirt got its name. *(from its T-shape)*

## Teacher Tip

For a home/school connection, assign one capital or lowercase letter to each child *(Aa, Bb, Tt)*. Ask children to look for their assigned letters after school as they ride to soccer practice, eat a snack in the kitchen, watch television, and so on. At school the next day, provide time for children to report where they saw their letter.

# Letter Recognition  Mm, Nn, Hh

## Objectives

- To recognize the letters *Mm*, *Nn*, and *Hh*
- To identify and sort different print styles and cases of *Mm*, *Nn*, and *Hh*

## Materials

 Big Book of Rhymes, Level K, "Ren's Nest," page 21

 Teacher Resource CD, Level K, Sort 9

 Word Study Notebook, Level K, pages 35–38

 *Words Their Way* Library, Level K, *The Farm*

 Teacher Resource CD, Level K, Alphabet Eggs game

### Letters

| Mm | Nn |
|---|---|
| 4 variations of *M* | 4 variations of *N* |
| 4 variations of *m* | 4 variations of *n* |

*Hh*
4 variations of *H*
4 variations of *h*

---

## Day 1 — Introduce the Sort

*Whole Group*

 **Read a Rhyme: "Ren's Nest"**

Read aloud "Ren's Nest" several times until children become familiar with the rhyme. Track the text as you read by pointing to each word. Next, read and track the first and second lines of the rhyme until children have memorized them. Call on volunteers to track these lines as you and the group read them aloud. When children have demonstrated that they can track accurately, encourage several volunteers to track specific words such as *eggs* and *nine*. Finally, have children search the poem to find examples of capital and lowercase *Mm*, *Nn,* and *Hh*.

 **Introduce Letter Sort *Mm, Nn, Hh***

Print out and cut apart the cards for Sort 9 from the Teacher Resource CD. Show the cards one at a time as you name each letter, and have children repeat the letter names. Then demonstrate how to sort the cards by letter names *Mm, Nn,* and *Hh*. As you sort the cards, point out the differences between *M* and *N* and between *m* and *n*. Ask how all the letters in a category are the same. Then ask how they are different.

## Day 2 — Practice the Sort

*Whole Group/Partner/Independent*

 You may want to begin Days 2–5 by rereading the rhyme from Day 1. Then review the previous day's sort. Help children tear out page 35 from their Word Study Notebook and cut apart the letter cards.

Have children work independently or with a partner to say the name of each letter and, using the grid on page 37 in their Word Study Notebook, sort the cards by letter names.

> **Alternative Sort: Straight or Curvy**
>
> When children are comfortable with this week's sort, suggest that they re-sort their letter cards, putting letters with straight lines only in one group and letters with curved lines in another group.

## Day 3

### Find Words in Context

*Whole Group*

Have children re-sort their cards. Then read aloud *The Farm* with children. Return to page 2, and ask a volunteer to point out a word that begins with *h*. *(house)* Repeat the process with *m* on page 3 *(mouse)*, and *n* on page 5. *(nail)* Continue by having children look for these letters within other words in the story.

## Day 4

### Apply the Skill

*Whole Group/Independent*

Have children sort their cards again. Then have them turn to page 38 in their Word Study Notebook. Read aloud the directions, and then guide children through the first few lines of the activity, demonstrating how to form the letters, if necessary. Let children complete the page on their own.

## Day 5

### Complete the Sort

*Whole Group/Independent*

**Paste in Place**

Have children turn to page 37 in their Word Study Notebook. Ask them to say the name of each letter at the top of the grid. Then have them sort their cards by letter name and paste the cards into the correct column for each letter.

**Play the Game**

When children are finished, they may play Alphabet Eggs. (See the Teacher Resource CD for game materials and playing directions.)

### ESL/ELL English Language Learners

Review the cards with children, naming each letter. Repeat the process, but have volunteers name the letters. Be sure children have their mouths positioned correctly as they say the letter names.

### Teacher Tip

If children are having problems identifying or forming the letters correctly, try providing tactile experiences. For example, let children use their fingers to trace letters cut from sandpaper.

# Letter Recognition  Cc, Dd, Ee

## Objectives

- To recognize the letters *Cc*, *Dd*, and *Ee*
- To identify and sort different print styles and cases of *Cc*, *Dd*, and *Ee*

## Materials

 Big Book of Rhymes, Level K, "Which Hat?," page 23

 Teacher Resource CD, Level K, Sort 10

 Word Study Notebook, Level K, pages 39–42

 *Words Their Way* Library, Level K, *The Hat*

 Teacher Resource CD, Level K, Concentration game

### Letters

| Cc | Dd |
|---|---|
| 4 variations of C | 4 variations of D |
| 4 variations of c | 4 variations of d |

Ee

4 variations of E

4 variations of e

---

### Introduce the Sort

*Whole Group*

 **Read a Rhyme: "Which Hat?"**

Read aloud "Which Hat?" several times until children become familiar with the rhyme. Track the text as you read by pointing to each word. Next, read and track the third and fourth lines of the rhyme until children have memorized them. Call on volunteers to track these lines as you and the group read them aloud. When children have demonstrated that they can track accurately, encourage several volunteers to track specific words such as *cook* and *do*. Finally, have children search the poem to find examples of capital and lowercase *Cc*, *Dd*, and *Ee*.

 **Introduce Letter Sort *Cc*, *Dd*, *Ee***

Print out and cut apart the cards for Sort 10. Introduce the cards, naming the letters. Then demonstrate how to sort the cards by letter names *Cc*, *Dd*, and *Ee*. Ask a volunteer to select a card from the first column, name the letter, and explain why the card is in that column. Continue with the other columns.

### Practice the Sort

*Whole Group/Partner/Independent*

 You may want to begin Days 2–5 by rereading the rhyme from Day 1. Then review the previous day's letter sort. Help children tear out page 39 from their Word Study Notebook and cut apart the letter cards.

Have children work independently or with a partner to say the name of each letter and, using the grid on page 41 in their Word Study Notebook, sort the cards by letter names.

#### Alternative Sort: Tall or Short

After children are comfortable with this week's sort, suggest that they re-sort their cards according to letter height. If needed, write the letters side-by-side on the board so that children can determine relative height. Have children make two piles, one for short letters and one for tall ones.

## Find Words in Context

*Whole Group*

Have children re-sort their cards. Then read aloud *The Hat* with children. Beginning with page 2, copy the words from the story onto the board. Let volunteers find and underline the letters *c, d,* and *e.* Point to the underlined letters, one at a time, as children call out the letter names.

## Apply the Skill

*Independent/Partner*

Have children sort their cards again. Then have them turn to page 42 in their Word Study Notebook. Read aloud the directions, and then let children work independently or with a partner to name and print the letters. If children are working with a partner, suggest that they take turns saying the letter name and writing the letter.

## Complete the Sort

*Whole Group/Independent*

### Paste in Place

Have children turn to page 41 in their Word Study Notebook. Ask them to say the name of each letter at the top of the grid. Then have them sort their cards by letter name and paste the cards into the correct column for each letter.

### Play the Game

When children are finished, they may play Concentration. (See the Teacher Resource CD for game materials and playing directions.)

ESL/ELL **English Language Learners**

Review the letter cards, naming each letter. Then stack the cards facedown, and ask children to guess the letter on the top card. Check pronunciation as children make their guesses. Turn over the card to see if any of children guessed correctly. Continue with the other cards in the stack.

## Teacher Tip

Reinforce learning by having children look for the letters *Cc, Dd,* and *Ee* throughout the school day. For example, when children are discussing the class calendar, ask if any of the letters are in the name of the month.

# Letter Recognition  Ee, Ff, Gg

## Objectives

- To recognize the letters *Ee*, *Ff*, and *Gg*
- To identify and sort different print styles and cases of *Ee*, *Ff*, and *Gg*

## Materials

 Big Book of Rhymes, Level K, "The Cook," page 25

 Teacher Resource CD, Level K, Sort 11

 Word Study Notebook, Level K, pages 43–46

 *Words Their Way* Library, Level K, *Eggs!*

 Teacher Resource CD, Level K, Bingo! game

| Letters | |
|---|---|
| *Ee* | *Ff* |
| 4 variations of *E* | 4 variations of *F* |
| 4 variations of *e* | 4 variations of *f* |
| *Gg* | |
| 4 variations of *G* | |
| 4 variations of *g* | |

---

## Day 1  Introduce the Sort

*Whole Group*

### Read a Rhyme: "The Cook"

Read aloud "The Cook" several times until children become familiar with the rhyme. Track the text as you read by pointing to each word. Next, read and track the fourth and fifth lines of the rhyme until children have memorized them. Call on volunteers to track these lines as you and the group read them aloud. When children have demonstrated that they can track accurately, encourage several volunteers to track specific words such as *flour* and *good*. Finally, have children search the poem to find examples of capital and lowercase *Ee*, *Ff*, and *Gg*.

### Introduce Letter Sort *Ee*, *Ff*, *Gg*

Print out and cut apart the letter cards for Sort 11. Show the cards as you name each letter. Ask which of the letters is repeated from last week's sort *(Ee)*, and point out the difference between *E* and *F*. Then demonstrate how to sort the cards by letter names *Ee*, *Ff*, and *Gg*. Discuss how the letters in a column are the same. Then ask how they are different.

## Day 2  Practice the Sort

*Whole Group/Partner/Independent*

You may want to begin Days 2–5 by rereading the rhyme from Day 1. Then review the previous day's sort. Help children tear out page 43 from their Word Study Notebook and cut apart the letter cards.

Have children work independently or with a partner to say the name of each letter and, using the grid on page 45 in their Word Study Notebook, sort the cards by letter names.

### Alternative Sort: The Starting Point

To reinforce the idea that proper names begin with capital letters, suggest that children re-sort their cards into two categories according to whether or not you would find the letter at the beginning of a person's name.

## Day 3

### Find Words in Context

*Whole Group*

Have children re-sort their cards. Then read aloud *Eggs!* with children. Then tell children that they will have a scavenger hunt to search for letters in the book. Provide a clue such as "*E* at the end of a word" or "A word with two *e*'s." Then leaf slowly through the pages of the book as children search for each letter. Invite them to point to the letters as they find them.

## Day 4

### Apply the Skill

*Independent/Partner*

Have children sort their cards again. Then have them turn to page 46 in their Word Study Notebook. Read aloud the directions, and then let children work independently or with a partner to name and print the letters. If children are working with a partner, suggest that they take turns, with one child naming and printing a capital letter and the other child naming and printing the corresponding lowercase letter.

## Day 5

### Complete the Sort

*Whole Group/Independent*

### Paste in Place

Have children turn to page 45 in their Word Study Notebook. Ask them to say the name of each letter at the top of the grid. Then have them sort their cards by letter name and paste the cards into the correct column for each letter.

### Play the Game

When children are finished, they may play Bingo! (See the Teacher Resource CD for game materials and playing directions.)

**ESL/ELL** **English Language Learners**

Bring a favorite recipe to class, printed on a recipe card. Help children practice conversation by talking about favorite foods. Then help children review the letter cards by naming the letters, one by one, and looking for them on the recipe card.

### Teacher Tip

Each week, have children search their classmates' names for the letters you are studying that week: "Who has the letter *f* in his or her name?" Keep track of which letters are used most frequently, and update the results on the board each week.

# Sort 12
# Letter Recognition Ii, Jj, Kk

## Objectives

- To recognize the letters *Ii*, *Jj*, and *Kk*
- To identify and sort different print styles and cases of *Ii*, *Jj*, and *Kk*

## Materials

 Big Book of Rhymes, Level K, "Jump!," page 27

 Teacher Resource CD, Level K, Sort 12

 Word Study Notebook, Level K, pages 47–50

 *Words Their Way* Library, Level K, *Jump Right In*

 Teacher Resource CD, Level K, Find the Letter game

| Letters | |
|---|---|
| *Ii* | *J* |
| 4 variations of *I* | 4 variations of *J* |
| 4 variations of *i* | 4 variations of *j* |
| *Kk* | |
| 4 variations of *K* | |
| 4 variations of *k* | |

## Day 1 — Introduce the Sort

*Whole Group*

 **Read a Rhyme: "Jump!"**

Read aloud "Jump!" several times until children become familiar with the rhyme. Track the text as you read by pointing to each word. Next, read and track the first and second lines of the rhyme until children have memorized them. Call on volunteers to track these lines as you and the group read them aloud. When children have demonstrated that they can track accurately, encourage several volunteers to track specific words such as *kangaroo* and *jump*. Finally, have children search the poem to find examples of capital and lowercase *Ii*, *Jj*, and *Kk*.

 **Introduce Letter Sort *Ii*, *Jj*, *Kk***

Print out and cut apart the letter cards for Sort 12 from the Teacher Resource CD. Introduce the cards, naming the letters. Then demonstrate for children how to sort the cards by letter names *Ii*, *Jj*, and *Kk*. As you sort the cards, discuss how the letters are alike and how they are different.

## Day 2 — Practice the Sort

*Whole Group/Partner/Independent*

 You may want to begin Days 2–5 by rereading the rhyme from Day 1. Then review the previous day's letter sort. Help children tear out page 47 from their Word Study Notebook and cut apart the letter cards.

Have children work independently or with a partner to say the name of each letter and, using the grid on page 49 in their Word Study Notebook, sort the cards by letter names.

### Alternative Sort: On the Dot

After children are comfortable with this week's sort, suggest that they re-sort their cards into two piles, one pile for dotted letters *(i, j)* and one pile for letters without dots *(I, J, K, k)*.

## Day 3

### Find Words in Context

*Whole Group*

Have children re-sort their cards. Then read aloud *Jump Right In* with children. Then reread pages 2, 3, and 8. Ask children how the words on the pages are alike. *(The words on pages 2 and 3 are the same as the words on page 8, except for A—B—C and X—Y—Z.)* Explain that the words are a chant that children repeat as they jump. Ask volunteers to identify the letters *J* and *i* in the chant. Then have children search for *J*, *i*, and *k* as you leaf through the rest of the book.

## Day 4

### Apply the Skill

*Independent/Partner*

Have children sort their cards again. Then have them turn to page 50 in their Word Study Notebook. Read aloud the directions. Let children work independently or with a partner to name and print the letters. If children are working in pairs, suggest that they take turns saying the letter name and writing the letter.

## Day 5

### Complete the Sort

*Whole Group/Independent*

### Paste in Place

Have children turn to page 49 in their Word Study Notebook. Ask them to say the name of each letter at the top of the grid. Then have them sort their cards by letter name and paste the cards into the correct column for each letter.

### Play the Game

When children are finished, they may play Find the Letter. (See the Teacher Resource CD for game materials and playing directions.)

**ESL/ELL** **English Language Learners**

Review the cards by having children name the letters after you. For practice in pronouncing the letters, teach children this variation of the chant in *Jump Right In.*

I—J—K

1—2—3

Jump right in.

Come play with me.

**Teacher Tip**

If children need additional practice forming letters, motivate them by inviting them to print the letters with colored pencils.

# Letter Recognition  Ll, Pp, Rr

## Objectives

- To recognize the letters *Ll*, *Pp*, and *Rr*
- To identify and sort different print styles and cases of *Ll*, *Pp*, and *Rr*

## Materials

 Big Book of Rhymes, Level K, "Look What We Can Do," page 29

 Teacher Resource CD, Level K, Sort 13

 Word Study Notebook, Level K, pages 51–54

 *Words Their Way* Library, Level K, *Pink Pig*

 Teacher Resource CD, Level K, Alphabet Eggs game

| Letters | |
|---|---|
| *Ll* | *Pp* |
| 4 variations of *L* | 4 variations of *P* |
| 4 variations of *l* | 4 variations of *p* |
| *Rr* | |
| 4 variations of *R* | |
| 4 variations of *r* | |

## Day 1  Introduce the Sort

*Whole Group*

### Read a Rhyme: "Look What We Can Do"

 Read aloud "Look What We Can Do" several times until children become familiar with the rhyme. Track the text as you read by pointing to each word. Next, read and track the third and fourth lines of the rhyme until children have memorized them. Call on volunteers to track these lines as you and the group read them aloud. When children have demonstrated that they can track accurately, encourage several volunteers to track specific words such as *can* and *play*. Finally, have children search the poem to find examples of capital and lowercase *Ll*, *Pp*, and *Rr*.

### Introduce Letter Sort Ll, Pp, Rr

 Print out and cut apart the letter cards for Sort 13 from the Teacher Resource CD. Show the cards and have children name each letter after you. Then demonstrate for children how to sort the cards by letter names *Ll*, *Pp*, and *Rr*. As you place the cards, ask how letters are alike or different from other letters in the same column.

## Day 2  Practice the Sort

*Whole Group/Partner/Independent*

 You may want to begin Days 2–5 by rereading the rhyme from Day 1. Then review the previous day's sort. Help children tear out page 51 from their Word Study Notebook and cut apart the letter cards.

Have children work independently or with a partner to say the name of each letter and, using the grid on page 53 in their Word Study Notebook, sort the cards by letter names.

### Alternative Sort: Capital or Lowercase

After children have completed this week's sort, have them sit on the floor next to a table. Have children re-sort their letters into two piles, a lower pile on the floor for lowercase letters and an upper pile on the table for capital, or uppercase, letters.

## Day 3

### Find Words in Context

*Whole Group*

Have children re-sort their cards. Then read aloud *Pink Pig* to children. Then reread the story, one sentence at a time, as children find and name *p*, *l*, and *r*. Challenge children to find one word that contains all three letters. *(purple on page 8)*

## Day 4

### Apply the Skill

*Independent/Partner*

Have children sort their cards again. Then have them turn to page 54 in their Word Study Notebook. Read aloud the directions, and have children work independently or with a partner to say and print the letters. If children are working in pairs, they should take turns doing the work and checking it.

## Day 5

### Complete the Sort

*Whole Group/Independent*

**Paste in Place**

Have children turn to page 53 in their Word Study Notebook. Ask them to say the name of each letter at the top of the grid. Then have them sort their cards by letter name and paste the cards into the correct column for each letter.

**Play the Game**

When children are finished, they may play Alphabet Eggs. (See the Teacher Resource CD for game materials and playing directions.)

**ESL/ELL English Language Learners**

Review the cards by having children repeat the letter names after you. Then use *Pink Pig* to practice pronunciation. Say the first phrase or word on each page, and have children say it after you.

### Teacher Tip

Periodically review letters from previous weeks. Have children take turns with a partner. Have one child write a letter and the other child say the letter name, or vice versa.

# Letter Recognition  Oo, Qq, Ss

## Objectives

- To recognize the letters *Oo, Qq,* and *Ss*
- To identify and sort different print styles and cases of *Oo, Qq,* and *Ss*

## Materials

 Big Book of Rhymes, Level K, "Quacks and Snacks," page 31

 Teacher Resource CD, Level K, Sort 14

 Word Study Notebook, Level K, pages 55–58

 *Words Their Way* Library, Level K, *Quack!*

 Teacher Resource CD, Level K, Match! game

### Letters

| Oo | Qq |
|---|---|
| 4 variations of O | 4 variations of Q |
| 4 variations of o | 4 variations of q |

Ss

4 variations of S

4 variations of s

---

## Day 1  Introduce the Sort

*Whole Group*

 **Read a Rhyme: "Quacks and Snacks"**

Read aloud "Quacks and Snacks" several times until children become familiar with the rhyme. Track the text as you read by pointing to each word. Next, read and track the third and fourth lines of the rhyme until children have memorized them. Call on volunteers to track these lines as you and the group read them aloud. When children have demonstrated that they can track accurately, encourage several volunteers to track specific words such as *quack* and *says.* Finally, have children search the poem to find examples of capital and lowercase *Oo, Qq,* and *Ss.*

 **Introduce Letter Sort Oo, Qq, Ss**

Print out and cut apart the cards for Sort 14. Show the cards as you name each letter. Compare the capital *Q* and *O*, pointing out the "tail" on the *Q*. Then demonstrate how to sort the cards by letter names *Oo, Qq,* and *Ss.* Ask volunteers to name the letters and tell if they are capital or lowercase.

## Day 2  Practice the Sort

*Whole Group/Partner/Independent*

 You may want to begin Days 2–5 by rereading the rhyme from Day 1. Then review the previous day's sort. Help children tear out page 55 from their Word Study Notebook and cut apart the letter cards.

Have children work independently or with a partner to say the name of each letter and, using the grid on page 57 in their Word Study Notebook, sort the cards by letter names.

### Alternative Sort: Circle Sort

After children are comfortable with this week's sort, suggest that they re-sort their cards into two piles according to whether or not the letter is shaped like a circle (or ellipse).

**Day 3**

## Find Words in Context

*Whole Group*

Have children re-sort their cards. Then read aloud *Quack!* to children. Tell children that they will be looking for the letter *q.* Leaf through the pages, and ask children to guess which page contains the most *q's.* (*Page 7 has seven.*) On the last page, ask volunteers to point out the letters *o* and *s.*

**Day 4**

## Apply the Skill

*Independent/Partner*

Have children sort their cards again. Then have them turn to page 58 in their Word Study Notebook. Read aloud the directions, and have children work independently or with a partner to name and print each letter. If children are working in pairs, suggest that children take turns saying the letter name and writing the letter.

**Day 5**

## Complete the Sort

*Whole Group/Independent*

### Paste in Place

Have children turn to page 57 in their Word Study Notebook. Ask them to say the name of each letter at the top of the grid. Then have them sort their cards by letter name and paste the cards into the correct column for each letter.

### Play the Game

When children are finished, they may play Match! (See the Teacher Resource CD for playing cards and directions.)

## ESL/ELL English Language Learners

Review the cards with children, naming each letter. Ask children what the ducks say in this week's poem and story. *(quack)* Write the word on the board and underline the *q.* Build vocabulary by asking children to name the sounds made by other animals, such as a cow, dog, rooster, owl, and so on.

## Teacher Tip

Circulate around the room to watch children as they print letters. Conventionally, most letter strokes are made from top to bottom, and most circular strokes are made counterclockwise.

# Letter Recognition Uu, Vv, Ww

## Objectives

- To recognize the letters *Uu*, *Vv*, and *Ww*
- To identify and sort different print styles and cases of *Uu*, *Vv*, and *Ww*

## Materials

 Big Book of Rhymes, Level K, "Vinny and the Bus," page 33

 Teacher Resource CD, Level K, Sort 15

 Word Study Notebook, Level K, pages 59–62

 *Words Their Way* Library, Level K, *Vultures on Vacation*

 Teacher Resource CD, Level K, Bingo! game

| Letters | |
|---|---|
| *Uu* | *Vv* |
| 4 variations of *U* | 4 variations of *V* |
| 4 variations of *u* | 4 variations of *v* |
| *Ww* | |
| 4 variations of *W* | |
| 4 variations of *w* | |

---

## Day 1 — Introduce the Sort

*Whole Group*

 **Read a Rhyme: "Vinny and the Bus"**

Read aloud "Vinny and the Bus" several times until children become familiar with the rhyme. Track the text as you read by pointing to each word. Next, read and track the first and second lines of the rhyme until children have memorized them. Call on volunteers to track these lines as you and the group read them aloud. When children have demonstrated that they can track accurately, encourage several volunteers to track specific words such as *us* and *sit*. Finally, have children search the poem to find examples of capital and lowercase *Uu*, *Vv*, and *Ww*.

 **Introduce Letter Sort *Uu*, *Vv*, *Ww***

Print out and cut apart the cards for Sort 15. Introduce the cards by having children name the letters after you. Then demonstrate how to sort the cards by letter names *Uu*, *Vv*, and *Ww*. Have volunteers name each letter, tell whether it is capital or lowercase, and explain why the card is in that column.

## Day 2 — Practice the Sort

*Whole Group/Partner/Independent*

 You may want to begin Days 2–5 by rereading the rhyme from Day 1. Then review the previous day's sort. Help children tear out page 59 from their Word Study Notebook and cut apart the letter cards.

Have children work independently or with a partner to say the name of each letter and, using the grid on page 61 in their Word Study Notebook, sort the cards by letter names.

### Alternative Sort: What Are Vowels?

After children have completed this week's sort, discuss the concept of vowels. Explain that only a few letters are vowels, but every word contains at least one. The letter *u* is one of the vowels. Have children sort their cards into two piles by whether or not the letter is a vowel.

## Day 3 — Find Words in Context

*Whole Group*

Have children re-sort their cards. Then read *Vultures on Vacation* to children. Have children name the animals in the story. *(vulture, fox, fish, kangaroo, hippo, walrus, jaguar)* List the animal names on the board. Ask children which animal name starts with the letter *v* or the letter *w*. *(vulture; walrus)* Help children find three animal names that contain the letter *u*. *(vulture, walrus, jaguar)*

## Day 4 — Apply the Skill

*Independent/Partner*

Have children sort their cards again. Then have them turn to page 62 in their Word Study Notebook. Read aloud the directions, and have children work independently or with a partner to complete the page. Remind children to say the names of the letters before they print them. If children are working in pairs, suggest that they take turns saying the letter name and writing the letter.

## Day 5 — Complete the Sort

*Whole Group/Independent*

### Paste in Place

Have children turn to page 61 in their Word Study Notebook. Ask them to say the name of each letter at the top of the grid. Then have them sort their cards by letter name and paste the cards into the correct column for each letter.

### Play the Game

When children are finished, they may play Bingo! (See the Teacher Resource CD for game materials and playing directions.)

## ESL/ELL English Language Learners

Review the cards with children, naming each letter. You may also want to review vocabulary from *Vultures on Vacation*. Discuss the illustrations with children, covering the key words on each page *(vulture/van, fox/fish, kangaroo/kite, hippo/hat, walrus/watch, jaguar/jar, vultures/vacation)*.

## Teacher Tip

As children sort their cards, circulate around the room asking questions and encouraging children to talk about the letters. For example, ask, "Why does this lowercase *v* go in the same column as these capital letters?" or "How can you tell whether this letter is a *v* or a *w*?"

# Letter Recognition Xx, Yy, Zz

## Objectives

- To recognize the letters *Xx, Yy,* and *Zz*
- To identify and sort different print styles and cases of *Xx, Yy,* and *Zz*

## Materials

 Big Book of Rhymes, Level K, "Come to the Zoo," page 35

 Teacher Resource CD, Level K, Sort 16

 Word Study Notebook, Level K, pages 63–66

 *Words Their Way* Library, Level K, *Good-bye, Zoo*

 Teacher Resource CD, Level K, Match the Letters game

### Letters

| Xx | Yy |
|---|---|
| 4 variations of *X* | 4 variations of *Y* |
| 4 variations of *x* | 4 variations of *y* |

| Zz |
|---|
| 4 variations of *Z* |
| 4 variations of *z* |

---

## Day 1 Introduce the Sort

*Whole Group*

 **Read a Rhyme: "Come to the Zoo"**

Read aloud "Come to the Zoo" several times until children become familiar with the rhyme. Track the text as you read by pointing to each word. Next, read and track the first and second lines of the rhyme until children have memorized them. Call on volunteers to track these lines as you and the group read them aloud. When children have demonstrated that they can track accurately, encourage several volunteers to track specific words such as *zoo* and *you*. Finally, have children search the poem to find examples of capital and lowercase *Xx, Yy,* and *Zz*.

 **Introduce Letter Sort *Xx, Yy, Zz***

Print out and cut apart the letter cards for Sort 16 from the Teacher Resource CD. Introduce the cards, naming the letters. Then demonstrate how to sort the cards by letter names *Xx, Yy,* and *Zz*. Ask children to describe how the letters in each column are alike and how they are different.

## Day 2 Practice the Sort

*Whole Group/Independent*

 You may want to begin Days 2–5 by rereading the rhyme from Day 1. Then review the previous day's sort. Help children tear out page 63 from their Word Study Notebook and cut apart the letter cards.

Have children work independently or with a partner to say the name of each letter. Then, using the grid on page 65 of their Word Study Notebook, have children sort their cards by letter names.

> **Alternative Sort: How Many Lines?**
>
> Once children are comfortable with this week's sort, re-sort the cards by letters made with two lines *(Xx, y)* and letters made with three lines *(Y, Zz)*. Point out that the capital Y and the lowercase y are made from a different number of lines.

50

**Day 3**

## Find Words in Context

*Whole Group/Independent*

Have children re-sort their cards. Then read aloud *Good-bye, Zoo*. Then take children on a "letter hunt" through the book to look for the letters *Yy* and *Zz*. Begin by asking children to locate their *Z* and *z* letter cards. Page through the book, pointing to various letters in the text. Have children hold up the appropriate card when you point to a *Z* or *z* in the text. Be sure to include letters that appear in the art as well. Repeat the procedure for *Y* and *y*.

**Day 4**

## Apply the Skill

*Independent/Partner*

Have children sort their cards again. Then have them turn to page 66 in their Word Study Notebook. Read aloud the directions, and have children work independently or with a partner to say the name of each letter and print it on the lines.

**Day 5**

## Complete the Sort

*Whole Group/Independent*

### Paste in Place

Have children turn to page 65 in their Word Study Notebook. Ask them to say the name of each letter at the top of the grid. Then have them sort their cards by letter name and paste the cards into the correct column for each letter.

### Play the Game

When children are finished, they may play Match the Letters. (See the Teacher Resource CD for playing cards and directions.)

**ESL/ELL** **English Language Learners**

Make sure children understand that the capital and lowercase letter pairs represent the same letter. To illustrate, use a child's name that contains both forms of the letter, such as Adam or Susan. Write the name on the board and circle the capital and lowercase letter pair. Point out that though the first occurrence of the letter is a capital letter and the second occurrence of the letter is a lowercase letter, they both have the same letter name.

## Teacher Tip

Children having difficulty recognizing the letters *Xx*, *Yy*, and *Zz* may benefit from tactile experiences. Provide a tray of salt or sand and the letter cards. Encourage children to take a card and trace the letter in the salt or sand while saying the letter name repeatedly. Others may benefit from an oral experience in which they create a chant or rhyme to help them remember each letter's shape.

 **Spell Check 2**

After completing Sorts 8–16, you may want to administer Spell Check 2 in the Word Study Notebook on page 148. See page 19 for instructions on progress monitoring and using the Spell Check.

# Sort 17
# Beginning Sounds  b, m

## Objectives

- To identify picture names beginning with the sounds of *b* and *m*
- To sort pictures by their beginning sound and associate each sound with the letter it represents

## Materials

 Big Book of Rhymes, Level K, "Bubbles," page 37

 Teacher Resource CD, Level K, Sort 17

 Word Study Notebook, Level K, pages 67–70

 *Words Their Way* Library, Level K, *Monster Mop*

Teacher Resource CD, Level K, Find the Picture game

| Pictures | |
|---|---|
| *b* | *m* |
| barn | man |
| bone | mule |
| ball | mop |
| bat | map |
| bed | moon |
| baby | milk |

## Day 1 Introduce the Sort

*Whole Group*

### Read a Rhyme: "Bubbles"

Read aloud "Bubbles" several times until children become familiar with the rhyme. Track the text as you read by pointing to each word. Next, read and track the third and fourth lines of the rhyme until children have memorized them. Call on volunteers to track these lines as you and the group read them aloud. When children have demonstrated that they can track accurately, encourage several volunteers to track specific words such as *big* and *mess*. Finally, have children search the poem to find examples of words that begin with the sound of *b* or *m*.

### Introduce Picture Sort *b, m*

Print out and cut apart the cards for Sort 17 from the Teacher Resource CD. Introduce the pictures, identifying *barn, moon, mule,* and any others that may be unfamiliar. Then demonstrate how to sort the pictures by the beginning sounds of their names. Have children say aloud each picture name and identify the letter that stands for each beginning sound.

## Day 2 Practice the Sort

*Whole Group/Independent/Partner*

You may want to begin Days 2–5 by rereading the rhyme from Day 1. Then review the previous day's sort. Help children tear out page 67 from their Word Study Notebook and cut apart the cards.

Have children work independently or with a partner to say each picture name and, using the grid on page 69 of their Word Study Notebook, sort the cards by their beginning sound.

### Alternative Sort: Knock on Wood

Once children are comfortable with this week's sort, ask them to think about what each item pictured might be made of. Then invite children to sort the cards according to whether or not the items pictured are often made of wood.

## Day 3

### Find Words in Context

*Whole Group/Independent*

Have children re-sort their cards. Then read *Monster Mop* with children. Have them listen for and identify words that begin with the sound of *m*. *(my, mat, mug, milk, mop)* After reading, help children look through their picture cards to find the two that match words in the text. *(milk, mop)* Lead children to understand that every word in the story begins with *m*.

## Day 4

### Apply the Skill

*Independent/Partner*

Have children sort their cards again. Then have them turn to page 70 in their Word Study Notebook. Read aloud the directions, and have children name the letters and pictures at the top of the page. Then have children work independently or with a partner to write the letters and draw pictures of things whose names begin like *bear* and *mouse*.

## Day 5

### Complete the Sort

*Whole Group/Independent*

#### Paste in Place

Have children turn to page 69 in their Word Study Notebook. Encourage them to say the name of each letter and picture at the top of the grid. Then have them sort their cards according to their beginning sounds and paste the pictures in place on the page.

#### Play the Game

When children are finished, they may play Find the Picture. (See the Teacher Resource CD for game materials and playing directions.)

## Building Vocabulary

Children may mistake the picture of a mule for that of a horse or a donkey. Explain that a mule has a horse for a mother and a donkey for a father; that is why it looks so much like both animals. Remind children that *mule* begins with the sound of *m*, while *horse* and *donkey* do not.

## ESL/ELL English Language Learners

Model using both lips to form the sound of *b*. Using words that start with *b* followed by a vowel, such as *baby*, helps to emphasize the formation and associated strong initial sound. The use of a mirror can help children check their mouth placement.

## Teacher Tip

As you work your way through Sorts 17 to 26 with children, you may want to use alphabet books to provide enrichment for the study of beginning consonant sounds. Distribute books to children, and ask them to work in pairs to find additional words that begin with each week's sounds.

# Beginning Sounds  r, s

## Objectives

- To identify picture names beginning with the sounds of *r* and *s*
- To sort pictures by their beginning sound and associate each sound with the letter it represents

## Materials

 Big Book of Rhymes, Level K, "The Raincoat," page 39

 Teacher Resource CD, Level K, Sort 18

 Word Study Notebook, Level K, pages 71–74

 *Words Their Way* Library, Level K, *Sandy*

 Teacher Resource CD, Level K, Go Fish game

### Pictures

| r | s |
|---|---|
| ring | six |
| road | seal |
| rope | sink |
| rocket | sock |
| rain | sun |
| roof | soap |

## Day 1 — Introduce the Sort

*Whole Group*

### Read a Rhyme: "The Raincoat"

Read aloud "The Raincoat" several times until children become familiar with the rhyme. Track the text as you read by pointing to each word. Next, read and track the first and second lines of the rhyme until children have memorized them. Call on volunteers to track these lines as you and the group read them aloud. When children have demonstrated that they can track accurately, encourage several volunteers to track specific words such as *ran* and *sun.* Finally, have children search the poem to find examples of words that begin with the sound of *r* or *s.*

### Introduce Picture Sort *r, s*

Print out and cut apart the cards for Sort 18. Introduce the pictures, identifying *six, road, rocket,* and any others that may be unfamiliar. Then demonstrate how to sort the pictures by the beginning sounds of their names. When the sort is complete, have children say aloud each picture name and identify the letter that stands for each beginning sound.

## Day 2 — Practice the Sort

*Whole Group/Independent/Partner*

You may want to begin Days 2–5 by rereading the rhyme from Day 1. Then review the previous day's sort. Help children tear out page 71 from their Word Study Notebook and cut apart the picture cards.

Have children work independently or with a partner to say each picture name and, using the grid on page 73 of their Word Study Notebook, sort the cards by their beginning sound.

### Alternative Sort: Inside or Outside

Once children are comfortable with the week's sort, invite them to sort the cards in a different way. Draw a picture of a house and a sun on the chalkboard. Explain to children that these are the column heads for things you find inside a house and things you find outside a house. Lead children as they sort the cards into the two categories.

## Find Words in Context

*Whole Group*

Have children re-sort their cards. Then read aloud *Sandy* with children. As you read each page, pause to allow children to identify words that begin with *r* or *s*. *(ran; Sandy, sat)*. You may choose to read the story twice, focusing on a different letter each time.

## Apply the Skill

*Independent/Partner*

Have children sort their cards again. Then have them turn to page 74 in their Word Study Notebook. Read aloud the directions, and have children name the letters and pictures at the top of the page. Then have children work independently or with a partner to write the letters and draw pictures of things whose names begin like *rock* and *saw*.

## Complete the Sort

*Whole Group/Independent*

### Paste in Place

Have children turn to page 73 in their Word Study Notebook. Encourage them to say the name of each letter and picture at the top of the grid. Then have them sort their cards according to their beginning sounds and paste the pictures in place on the page.

### Play the Game

When children are finished, they may play Go Fish. (See the Teacher Resource CD for playing cards and directions.)

## Building Vocabulary

Children may be unfamiliar with the term *rocket* or mistake the picture for a space shuttle. Explain that a rocket was used to transport people into space in the early days of space travel, before the space shuttle was invented.

## ESL/ELL English Language Learners

Ask children having difficulty pronouncing the sound of *r* to pretend to be a lion. Model how to roar, stretching the beginning sound *(rrrrroar)*. Encourage children to do the same.

## Teacher Tip

As a challenge activity, have children write the letters *r* and *s* on self-stick notes and attach them to items in the classroom whose names begin with the corresponding sound. Children may also enjoy brainstorming a list of words that begin with *s* and incorporating them into a tongue twister.

# Sort 19

# Beginning Sounds  t, g

## Objectives

- To identify picture names beginning with the sounds of *t* and *g*
- To sort pictures by their beginning sound and associate each sound with the letter it represents

## Materials

Big Book of Rhymes, Level K, "Tubby Turtle," page 41

Teacher Resource CD, Level K, Sort 19

Word Study Notebook, Level K, pages 75–78

*Words Their Way* Library, Level K, *Nanny Goat's Nap*

Teacher Resource CD, Level K, Bingo! game

### Pictures

| t | g |
|---|---|
| tie | gift |
| toe | gate |
| tooth | girl |
| tire | goose |
| top | game |
| toys | goat |

---

## Day 1 — Introduce the Sort

*Whole Group*

### Read a Rhyme: "Tubby Turtle"

Read aloud "Tubby Turtle" several times until children become familiar with the rhyme. Track the text as you read by pointing to each word. Next, read and track the first and second lines of the rhyme until children have memorized them. Call on volunteers to track these lines as you and the group read them aloud. When children have demonstrated that they can track accurately, encourage several volunteers to track specific words such as *turtle* and *good*. Finally, have children search the poem to find examples of words that begin with the sound of *t* or *g*.

### Introduce Picture Sort *t, g*

Print out and cut apart the cards for Sort 19. Introduce the pictures, identifying *top, gift, gate*, and any others that may be unfamiliar. Then demonstrate how to sort the pictures by the beginning sounds of their names. When the sort is complete, have children say aloud each picture name and identify the letter that stands for each beginning sound.

## Day 2 — Practice the Sort

*Whole Group/Independent/Partner*

You may want to begin Days 2–5 by rereading the rhyme from Day 1. Then review the previous day's sort. Help children tear out page 75 from their Word Study Notebook and cut apart the cards.

Have children work independently or with a partner to say each picture name and, using the grid on page 77 of their Word Study Notebook, sort the cards by their beginning sound.

> **Alternative Sort: Now Hear This**
> Once children are comfortable with the week's sort, invite them to sort the cards into two groups—things that make noise and things that are quiet. After children have sorted their pictures, encourage them to describe the sound made by each thing in the noisy group.

## Day 3 — Find Words in Context

*Whole Group/Independent*

Have children re-sort their cards. Then tell children that this week's poem and book are both about a goat. Remind them that *goat* starts with *g*. As you read *Nanny Goat's Nap*, have children listen for and identify words that begin with *g* and *t*. (*Goat, Goose, Grasshopper, garden, good; take, tree*) After reading, help children look through their picture cards to find the two that match words in the text. (*goat, goose*) Read the story again, and have children hold up the appropriate card when they hear the word in the text.

## Day 4 — Apply the Skill

*Independent/Partner*

Have children sort their cards again. Then have them turn to page 78 in their Word Study Notebook. Read aloud the directions, and have children name the letters and pictures at the top of the page. Then have children work independently or with a partner to write the letters and draw pictures of things whose names begin like *tiger* and *gum*.

## Day 5 — Complete the Sort

*Whole Group/Independent*

### Paste in Place

Have children turn to page 77 in their Word Study Notebook. Encourage them to say the name of each letter and picture at the top of the grid. Then have them sort their cards according to their beginning sounds and paste the pictures in place on the page.

### Play the Game

When children are finished, they may play Bingo! (See the Teacher Resource CD for game materials and playing directions.)

## Building Vocabulary

Children may not recognize the picture of a top. Explain that the top in the picture is a kind of toy that spins. Remind children that the word *top* has several other meanings, and ask them to volunteer any that they might know.

## ESL/ELL English Language Learners

After helping children sort the words according to beginning sound, have them pronounce the picture names that begin with *t*. Check to be sure they are saying the sound for *t* rather than for *d*. To help them, have them hold their hands in front of their lips as they pronounce the words. Explain that they should feel a puff of air on their hands as they say the first sound in each word.

## Teacher Tip

If children are unable to sort a card by its beginning sound, give them this tip. Children should say the first picture name at the top of the grid (*tiger*), and then the picture card name (*tire*). Children should then repeat with the second picture at the top of the grid (*gum, tire*). This will help children match beginning sounds and complete the sort.

# Sort 20

# Beginning Sounds  n, p

## Objectives

- To identify picture names beginning with the sounds of *n* and *p*
- To sort pictures by their beginning sound and associate each sound with the letter it represents

## Materials

 Big Book of Rhymes, Level K, "The Best Homes," page 43

 Teacher Resource CD, Level K, Sort 20

 Word Study Notebook, Level K, pages 79–82

 *Words Their Way* Library, Level K, *Where Is It?*

 Teacher Resource CD, Level K, Around the Farm game

### Pictures

| n | p |
|---|---|
| nap | parrot |
| net | pin |
| nose | pillow |
| nest | pig |
| nail | pen |
| nurse | peach |

## Day 1 — Introduce the Sort

*Whole Group*

 **Read a Rhyme: "The Best Homes"**

Read aloud "The Best Homes" several times until children become familiar with the rhyme. Track the text as you read by pointing to each word. Next, read and track the first and second lines of the rhyme until children have memorized them. Call on volunteers to track these lines as you and the group read them aloud. When children have demonstrated that they can track accurately, encourage several volunteers to track specific words such as *pen* and *nest*. Finally, have children search the poem to find examples of words that begin with the sound of *n* or *p*.

 **Introduce Picture Sort n, p**

Print out and cut apart the cards for Sort 20. Introduce the pictures, identifying *net, parrot, nurse,* and any others that may be unfamiliar. Then demonstrate how to sort the pictures by the beginning sounds of their names. When the sort is complete, have children say aloud each picture name and identify the letter that stands for each beginning sound.

## Day 2 — Practice the Sort

*Whole Group/Independent/Partner*

 You may want to begin Days 2–5 by rereading the rhyme from Day 1. Then review the previous day's sort. Help children tear out page 79 from their Word Study Notebook and cut apart the cards.

Have children work independently or with a partner to say each picture name and, using the grid on page 81 of their Word Study Notebook, sort the cards by their beginning sound.

**Alternative Sort: State the Weight**

Once children are comfortable with the week's sort, review the concepts of heavy and light. Then have children sort the picture cards by things that are heavy and things that are light. Encourage children to explain their reasoning.

58

## Day 3

### Find Words in Context

*Whole Group/Independent*

Have children re-sort their cards. Then read *Where Is It?* with children. Ask them to listen for words that begin like *nap* or *pot*. Discuss the pictures in the book. Have children look through their picture cards and find those that match the photographs in the book. *(pig, net, nest)* You may want to discuss the two different meanings of the word *pen*.

## Day 4

### Apply the Skill

*Independent/Partner*

Have children sort their cards again. Then have them turn to page 82 in their Word Study Notebook. Read aloud the directions, and have children name the letters and pictures at the top of the page. Then have children work independently or with a partner to write the letters and draw pictures of things whose names begin like *nut* and *pot*.

## Day 5

### Complete the Sort

*Whole Group/Independent*

#### Paste in Place

Have children turn to page 81 in their Word Study Notebook. Encourage them to say the name of each letter and picture at the top of the grid. Then have them sort their cards according to their beginning sounds and paste the pictures in place on the page.

#### Play the Game

When children are finished, they may play Around the Farm. (See the Teacher Resource CD for game materials and playing directions.)

## Building Vocabulary

If children mistake the *parrot* picture card for *bird*, remind them that a parrot is a type of bird whose name begins with the *p* sound. Ask children whether or not they've ever seen a live parrot before, and if so, to describe the experience.

## ESL/ELL English Language Learners

Pair English language learners with children who are proficient in the language. Have each pair play Copy Cat. Using the picture cards, have the English language learner pick a card and show it to his or her partner, who should say the word slowly. The English language learner should then repeat the word. Have children use the same procedure for the remaining cards. Then have partners go through the cards again at a more rapid pace. Listen and provide guidance as necessary.

## Teacher Tip

Letter formation may be difficult for children as they complete page 82 in their Word Study Notebook. Consider creating a chant or rhyme to help children remember the proper strokes to form each letter. While you should not expect perfection, you should encourage both proper handwriting techniques and attempts.

59

# Sort 21
# Beginning Sounds  c, h

## Objectives

- To identify picture names beginning with the sounds of *c* and *h*
- To sort pictures by their beginning sound and associate each sound with the letter it represents

## Materials

 Big Book of Rhymes, Level K, "Farm Friends," page 45

 Teacher Resource CD, Level K, Sort 21

 Word Study Notebook, Level K, pages 83–86

 *Words Their Way* Library, Level K, *On the Farm*

 Teacher Resource CD, Level K, Find the Picture game

### Pictures

| c | h |
|---|---|
| can | hand |
| carrot | ham |
| cow | hay |
| camel | horse |
| cape | hot |
| candle | hat |

## Day 1 — Introduce the Sort

*Whole Group*

 **Read a Rhyme: "Farm Friends"**

Read aloud "Farm Friends" several times until children become familiar with the rhyme. Track the text as you read by pointing to each word. Next, read and track the fifth and sixth lines of the rhyme until children have memorized them. Call on volunteers to track these lines as you and the group read them aloud. When children have demonstrated that they can track accurately, encourage several volunteers to track specific words such as *can* and *here*. Finally, have children search the poem to find examples of words that begin with the sound of *c* or *h*.

 **Introduce Picture Sort *c, h***

Print out and cut apart the cards for Sort 21. Introduce the pictures, identifying *cape, ham, camel,* and any others that may be unfamiliar. Then demonstrate how to sort the pictures by the beginning sounds of their names. When the sort is complete, have children say aloud each picture name and identify the letter that stands for the beginning sound.

## Day 2 — Practice the Sort

*Whole Group/Independent/Partner*

 You may want to begin Days 2–5 by rereading the rhyme from Day 1. Then review the previous day's sort. Help children tear out page 83 from their Word Study Notebook and cut apart the cards.

Have children work independently or with a partner to say each picture name and, using the grid on page 85 of their Word Study Notebook, sort the cards by their beginning sound.

### Alternative Sort: Growing Up

Once children are comfortable completing the week's sort, lead them in another sorting activity. Remind children that living things grow and change over time. Ask children to sort the pictures into things that grow and things that do not grow. Encourage children to explain their reasoning, and provide guidance as necessary.

## Find Words in Context

*Whole Group/Independent*

Have children re-sort their cards. Then introduce *On the Farm* by telling children that a word beginning with the *h* sound appears on every page of the book. Read page 2 and ask children to identify the word that begins like *hot. (have)* Point out the word on the page. Pause after reading each page, and have children locate the word *have* and isolate its beginning sound. Page through the book again, and have children identify the two pictures whose names begin with *c. (cows, corn)* Help children find the picture card that matches a picture in the book. *(cow)*

## Apply the Skill

*Independent/Partner*

Have children sort their cards again. Then have them turn to page 86 in their Word Study Notebook. Read aloud the directions, and have children name the letters and pictures at the top of the page. Then have children work independently or with a partner to write the letters and draw pictures of things whose names begin like *cup* and *hen.*

## Complete the Sort

*Whole Group/Independent*

### Paste in Place

Have children turn to page 85 in their Word Study Notebook. Encourage them to say the name of each letter and picture at the top of the grid. Then have them sort their cards according to their beginning sounds and paste the pictures in place on the page.

### Play the Game

When children are finished, they may play Find the Picture. (See the Teacher Resource CD for game materials and playing directions.)

## Building Vocabulary

If children are unfamiliar with the word *cape,* explain that it is a type of coat that doesn't have sleeves and is fastened at the neck. Discuss with children how the picture card for *cape* might help them understand the word's meaning.

## ESL/ELL English Language Learners

Model how to correctly pronounce the beginning sound of *c* as in *cup.* Teach children how to exhale and squeeze their abdominal muscles in order to emphasize the sound. As children focus on the pronunciation of one sound, such as *c,* ignore incorrect pronunciations of other sounds, to help prevent feelings of inadequacy.

## Teacher Tip

Listen as children complete the sorting activities. Check their pronunciations and their ability to isolate and discriminate among the beginning sounds in the sort. Provide individual guidance and reinforcement when necessary.

# Beginning Sounds  f, d

## Objectives

- To identify picture names beginning with the sounds of *f* and *d*
- To sort pictures by their beginning sound and associate each sound with the letter it represents

## Materials

Big Book of Rhymes, Level K, "Dancing Clown," page 47

Teacher Resource CD, Level K, Sort 22

Word Study Notebook, Level K, pages 87–90

*Words Their Way* Library, Level K, *Funny Faces and Funny Places*

Teacher Resource CD, Level K, Pair It game

| Pictures | |
|---|---|
| *f* | *d* |
| fish | deer |
| fire | desk |
| fan | duck |
| fox | doll |
| foot | dog |
| feather | dinosaur |

---

## Day 1 Introduce the Sort

*Whole Group*

### Read a Rhyme: "Dancing Clown"

Read aloud "Dancing Clown" several times until children become familiar with the rhyme. Track the text as you read by pointing to each word. Next, read and track the first and second lines of the rhyme until children have memorized them. Call on volunteers to track these lines as you and the group read them aloud. When children have demonstrated that they can track accurately, encourage several volunteers to track specific words such as *dance* and *fancy*. Finally, have children search the poem to find examples of words that begin with the sound of *f* or *d*.

### Introduce Picture Sort *f, d*

Print out and cut apart the cards for Sort 22. Introduce the pictures, identifying *fox, dog, fire*, and any others that might be unfamiliar. Then demonstrate how to sort the pictures by the beginning sounds of their names. When the sort is complete, have children say aloud each picture name and identify the letter that stands for each beginning sound.

## Day 2 Practice the Sort

*Whole Group/Independent/Partner*

You may want to begin Days 2–5 by rereading the rhyme from Day 1. Then review the previous day's sort demonstration with children. Help children tear out page 87 from their Word Study Notebook and cut apart the picture cards.

Have children work independently or with a partner to say each picture name and, using the grid on page 89 of their Word Study Notebook, sort the cards by their beginning sound.

### Alternative Sort: Animals All Around

Once children are comfortable completing the week's sort, ask them to sort the cards into pictures of animals and pictures of other things. Then say other words that begin with *f* and *d*, such as *fence, ferret,* and *dish*, and ask children to tell which category they belong in.

## Day 3

### Find Words in Context

*Whole Group*

Have children re-sort their cards. Then show children the cover of *Funny Faces and Funny Places*. Ask children to predict what the story will be about. Read the title of the book, and point out the words that begin with *f*. As you read, ask children to listen for the repeated phrase *funny faces*. Reread the story, and have children raise their hand when they hear a word that begins with *d*. *(down)*

## Day 4

### Apply the Skill

*Independent/Partner*

Have children sort their cards again. Then have them turn to page 90 in their Word Study Notebook. Read aloud the directions, and have children name the letters and pictures at the top of the page. Then have children work independently or with a partner to write the letters and draw pictures of things whose names begin like *fork* and *dime*.

## Day 5

### Complete the Sort

*Whole Group/Independent*

**Paste in Place**

Have children turn to page 89 in their Word Study Notebook. Encourage them to say the name of each letter and picture at the top of the grid. Then have them sort their cards according to their beginning sounds and paste the pictures in place on the page.

**Play the Game**

When children are finished, they may play Pair It. (See the Teacher Resource CD for game materials and playing directions.)

## Building Vocabulary

Some children may think that the *fox* picture card shows a dog. Explain that a fox is similar to a dog, but that it is a wild animal. Encourage children who have seen foxes at a zoo or in the wild to share their experience.

## ESL/ELL English Language Learners

Children learning a language benefit from hearing new words in context. When introducing the pictures for this week's sort, use each word in a sentence. Invite children to repeat the word and your example sentence, and then use the word in a sentence of their own.

## Teacher Tip

Encourage children to brainstorm other words that begin with *f* or *d*. Invite them to draw pictures of the words and incorporate them into the sort.

# Sort 23

# Beginning Sounds  l, k

## Objectives

- To identify picture names beginning with the sounds of *l* and *k*
- To sort pictures by their beginning sound and associate each sound with the letter it represents

## Materials

Big Book of Rhymes, Level K, "Four Little Kittens," page 49

Teacher Resource CD, Level K, Sort 23

Word Study Notebook, Level K, pages 91–94

*Words Their Way* Library, Level K, *Little Kittens*

Teacher Resource CD, Level K, Kittens in the Kitchen game

### Pictures

| l | k |
|---|---|
| lips | kite |
| lizard | kitten |
| lamp | kitchen |
| leaf | kangaroo |
| lock | key |
| lion | king |

## Day 1 · Introduce the Sort

*Whole Group*

### Read a Rhyme: "Four Little Kittens"

Read aloud "Four Little Kittens" several times until children become familiar with the rhyme. Track the text as you read by pointing to each word. Next, read and track the first and second lines of the rhyme until children have memorized them. Call on volunteers to track these lines as you and the group read them aloud. When children have demonstrated that they can track accurately, encourage several volunteers to track specific words such as *kitten* and *lazy*. Finally, have children search the poem to find examples of words that begin with the sound of *l* or *k*.

### Introduce Picture Sort l, k

Print out and cut apart the cards for Sort 23. Introduce the pictures, identifying *lizard, lock, kitchen*, and any others that may be unfamiliar. Then demonstrate how to sort the pictures by the beginning sounds of their names. When the sort is complete, have children say aloud each picture name and identify the letter that stands for each beginning sound.

## Day 2 · Practice the Sort

*Whole Group/Independent/Partner*

You may want to begin Days 2–5 by rereading the rhyme from Day 1. Then review the previous day's sort demonstration with children. Help children tear out page 91 from their Word Study Notebook and cut apart the picture cards.

Have children work independently or with a partner to say each picture name and, using the grid on page 93 of their Word Study Notebook, sort the cards by their beginning sound.

### Alternative Sort: Up So High

Once children are comfortable completing the week's sort, invite them to sort the cards into different categories. Ask children to say each picture name and decide if it is something they might see in the air. If it is, have them put the card in one column. If not, have them put it in a separate column. Encourage children to explain their reasoning.

## Day 3

### Find Words in Context

*Whole Group/Independent*

Have children re-sort their cards. Then read the title of *Little Kittens* to children. Ask children which word in the title begins with *l* and which word begins with *k*. Ask children to listen for more words that begin with *l* or *k* as you read the text aloud. Have children look through their picture cards and find the one that matches a picture in the book. *(kitten)*

## Day 4

### Apply the Skill

*Independent/Partner*

Have children sort their cards again. Then have them turn to page 94 in their Word Study Notebook. Read aloud the directions, and have children name the letters and pictures at the top of the page. Then have children work independently or with a partner to write the letters and draw pictures of things whose names begin like *log* and *kick*.

## Day 5

### Complete the Sort

*Whole Group/Independent*

#### Paste in Place

Have children turn to page 93 in their Word Study Notebook. Encourage them to say the name of each letter and picture at the top of the grid. Then have them sort their cards according to their beginning sounds and paste the pictures in place on the page.

#### Play the Game

When children are finished, they may play Kittens in the Kitchen. (See the Teacher Resource CD for game materials and playing directions.)

## Building Vocabulary

Children may have trouble determining which picture card shows a *lock* and which shows a *key*. Explain that a lock is something that keeps a door, lid, or other object fastened, and a key is something that lets you open the lock.

### ESL/ELL English Language Learners

Ask children to say the word *lamp* and describe what they feel in their mouth as they make the first sound. Tell children that to pronounce the initial *l*, they should put the tip of their tongue on the roof of their mouth right behind the top teeth and let air pass around their tongue. Repeat with the word *key*. Explain that to make the sound of initial *k*, children should put the back of their tongue on the roof of their mouth.

## Teacher Tip

Make a clear distinction between letter names and letter sounds. Point out that sometimes the letter names can give you a clue as to the letter sounds. For example, the sound of *k* is heard at the beginning of the letter name. Likewise, the sound of *l* is heard at the end of the letter name.

# Beginning Sounds j, w, q

## Objectives

- To identify picture names beginning with the sounds of *j*, *w*, and *q*
- To sort pictures by their beginning sound and associate each sound with the letter it represents

## Materials

Big Book of Rhymes, Level K, "My Jeans," page 51

Teacher Resource CD, Level K, Sort 24

Word Study Notebook, Level K, pages 95–98

*Words Their Way* Library, Level K, *For Sale*

Teacher Resource CD, Level K, Bingo! game

### Pictures

| *j* | *w* |
|-----|-----|
| jar | wing |
| jacket | web |
| jeans | wave |
| jet | wagon |
| jump | wig |

*q*
quilt
quack
question
quarter
quiet

---

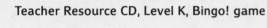

## Day 1 — Introduce the Sort

*Whole Group*

### Read a Rhyme: "My Jeans"

Read aloud "My Jeans" several times until children become familiar with the rhyme. Track the text as you read by pointing to each word. Next, read and track the first and second lines of the rhyme until children have memorized them. Call on volunteers to track these lines as you and the group read them aloud. When children have demonstrated that they can track accurately, encourage several volunteers to track specific words such as *jeans* and *way*. Finally, have children search the poem to find examples of words that begin with the sound of *j*, *w*, or *q*.

### Introduce Picture Sort *j, w, q*

Print out and cut apart the cards for Sort 24. Introduce the pictures, identifying *quack, quilt, question*, and any others that might be unfamiliar. Then demonstrate how to sort the pictures by the beginning sounds of their names. When the sort is complete, have children say aloud each picture name and identify the letter that stands for each beginning sound.

## Day 2 — Practice the Sort

*Whole Group/Independent/Partner*

You may want to begin Days 2–5 by rereading the rhyme from Day 1. Then review the previous day's sort. Help children tear out page 95 from their Word Study Notebook and cut apart the picture cards.

Have children work independently or with a partner to say each picture name and, using the grid on page 97 of their Word Study Notebook, sort the cards by their beginning sound.

### Alternative Sort: Handheld

Once children are comfortable completing the week's sort, have them sort the cards into pictures of items that can be held with one or two hands and pictures of items that can't be held.

## Day 3 — Find Words in Context

*Whole Group/Independent*

Have children re-sort their cards. Then read *For Sale* with children. On a second reading, make a list on the board of the words in the book that begin with *j (jackets, jeans)* and *w (We, wigs, watches)*. Read each word in the list, calling attention to the beginning letter and sound. Ask children to find two picture cards that match pictures in the book. *(jacket, wig)*

## Day 4 — Apply the Skill

*Independent/Partner*

Have children sort their cards again. Then have them turn to page 98 in their Word Study Notebook. Read aloud the directions, and have children name the letters and pictures at the top of the page. Then have children work independently or with a partner to write the letters and draw pictures of things whose names begin like *jeep, watch,* and *queen.*

## Day 5 — Complete the Sort

*Whole Group/Independent*

### Paste in Place

Have children turn to page 96 in their Word Study Notebook. Encourage them to say the name of each letter and picture at the top of the grid. Then have them sort their cards according to their beginning sounds and paste the pictures in place on the page.

### Play the Game

When children are finished, they may play Bingo! (See the Teacher Resource CD for game materials and playing directions.)

## Building Vocabulary

Help children understand the meaning of the word *question* by explaining that it is a sentence that asks for something. Display the picture card, and tell them that it shows a question mark—a kind of punctuation that is always found at the end of a question.

## ESL/ELL English Language Learners

English language learners may assume that words like *queen* and *quack* begin with the letter *k*. Point out that the beginning sound in words beginning with *q* is actually /kw/. Read aloud the names of the picture cards that begin with *q*, drawing out the beginning sound, and have children repeat the names after you.

## Teacher Tip

Encourage children to play a form of I Spy by looking and listening for the week's beginning sounds as they travel to and from school. Give children an opportunity to describe any encounters they have with the sounds.

# Beginning Sounds  y, z, v

## Objectives

- To identify picture names beginning with the sounds of *y*, *z*, and *v*
- To sort pictures by their beginning sound and associate each sound with the letter it represents

## Materials

Big Book of Rhymes, Level K, "Seeing Yellow," page 53

Teacher Resource CD, Level K, Sort 25

Word Study Notebook, Level K, pages 99–102

*Words Their Way* Library, Level K, *Zebra's Yellow Van*

Teacher Resource CD, Level K, Concentration game

### Pictures

| y | z |
|---|---|
| yell | zoo |
| yarn | zebra |
| yogurt | zero |
| yo-yo | zucchini |
| yard | zigzag |

**v**
vest
van
vine
violin
vase

---

## Day 1 — Introduce the Sort

*Whole Group*

### Read a Rhyme: "Seeing Yellow"

Read aloud "Seeing Yellow" several times until children become familiar with the rhyme. Track the text as you read by pointing to each word. Next, read and track the third and fourth lines of the rhyme until children have memorized them. Call on volunteers to track these lines as you and the group read them aloud. When children have demonstrated that they can track accurately, encourage several volunteers to track specific words such as *zips* and *van*. Finally, have children search the poem to find examples of words that begin with the sound of *y*, *z*, or *v*.

### Introduce Picture Sort y, z, v

Print out and cut apart the cards for Sort 25. Introduce the pictures, identifying *vine, zucchini, zigzag,* and any others that might be unfamiliar. Then demonstrate how to sort the pictures by the beginning sounds of their names. When the sort is complete, have children say aloud each picture name and identify the letter that stands for each beginning sound.

## Day 2 — Practice the Sort

*Whole Group/Independent/Partner*

You may want to begin Days 2–5 by rereading the rhyme from Day 1. Then review the previous day's sort. Help children tear out page 99 from their Word Study Notebook and cut apart the cards.

Have children work independently or with a partner to say each picture name and, using the grid on page 101 of their Word Study Notebook, sort the cards by their beginning sound.

> ### Alternative Sort: Beats in a Word
> When children are comfortable completing the week's sort, lead them in a sort according to the number of beats (one, two, or three) in the word. Say each picture name with children, clapping each beat as you do so. After the sort, have children identify the beginning sound in each word.

## Day 3 — Find Words in Context

*Whole Group/Independent*

Have children re-sort their cards. Then read the title of *Zebra's Yellow Van*. Review beginning sounds *y*, *z*, and *v*. Ask children which word in the title begins with *y*, and repeat for *z* and *v*. Repeat the routine when you read pages 2, 4, and 6. Have children listen for and name the word that begins like *zebra* on page 7 *(zoo)* and the word that begins like *yellow* on page 8 *(yes)*. Ask children to look through their cards and find the three that match pictures in the book. *(zebra, van, zoo)*

## Day 4 — Apply the Skill

*Independent/Partner*

Have children sort their cards again. Then have them turn to page 102 in their Word Study Notebook. Read aloud the directions, and have children name the letters and pictures at the top of the page. Then have children work independently or with a partner to write the letters and draw pictures of things whose names begin like *yawn*, *zipper*, and *volcano*.

## Day 5 — Complete the Sort

*Whole Group/Independent*

### Paste in Place

Have children turn to page 101 in their Word Study Notebook. Encourage them to say the name of each letter and picture at the top of the grid. Then have them sort their cards according to their beginning sounds and paste the pictures in place on the page.

### Play the Game

When children are finished, they may play Concentration. (See the Teacher Resource CD for game materials and playing directions.)

## Building Vocabulary

Children may confuse the zucchini in their picture card with a cucumber, or they may not be familiar with the vegetable at all. Explain that a zucchini is a kind of vegetable called a squash and that many people like to grow zucchinis in their garden. Encourage children who have eaten zucchini to describe what it tastes like and how it can be prepared.

## ESL/ELL English Language Learners

You may want to use a different technique to have children complete the sort. Model how to say *yawn*, one of the picture names at the top of the sorting grid. Then go through the cards, saying each picture name and listening only for words that have the same beginning sound as *yawn*. Continue with *zipper* and *volcano*, the other two words at the top of the sorting grid.

## Teacher Tip

Some children may benefit from a more tactile experience. Provide children with pencils, toothpicks, or other straight objects. Encourage children to use the items to create the letters whose beginning sounds are represented in the sort. Ask children to identify each completed letter by its name and sound. As a final step, children can review the picture cards and say the picture names for each completed letter.

# Ending Sounds t, x

## Sort 26

## Objectives

- To identify picture names ending with the sounds of *t* and *x*
- To sort pictures by their ending sound and associate each sound with the letter it represents

## Materials

Big Book of Rhymes, Level K, "Fox in a Box," page 55

Teacher Resource CD, Level K, Sort 26

Word Study Notebook, Level K, pages 103–106

*Words Their Way* Library, Level K, *Fix It, Fox*

Teacher Resource CD, Level K, Fine the Picture game

### Pictures

| *t* | *x* |
|-----|-----|
| hit | fox |
| jet | ox |
| pot | six |
| cat | wax |
| sit | box |
| dot | mix |

## Day 1 — Introduce the Sort

*Whole Group*

### Read a Rhyme: "Fox in a Box"

Read aloud "Fox in a Box" several times until children become familiar with the rhyme. Track the text as you read by pointing to each word. Next, read and track the first and second lines of the rhyme until children have memorized them. Call on volunteers to track these lines as you and the group read them aloud. When children have demonstrated that they can track accurately, encourage several volunteers to track specific words such as *box* and *cat*. Finally, have children search the poem to find examples of words that end with the sound of *t* or *x*.

### Introduce Picture Sort *t, x*

Print out and cut apart the cards for Sort 26. Introduce the pictures, identifying *ox, wax, dot,* and any others that may be unfamiliar. Then demonstrate how to sort the pictures by ending sounds *t* and *x*. Ask children to say aloud each picture name and identify the letter that stands for each ending sound.

## Day 2 — Practice the Sort

*Whole Group/Independent/Partner*

You may want to begin Days 2–5 by rereading the rhyme from Day 1. Then, review the previous day's sort. Help children tear out page 103 from their Word Study Notebook and cut apart the picture cards.

Have children work independently or with a partner to say each picture name and, using the grid on page 105 of their Word Study Notebook, sort the picture cards by ending sounds.

### Alternative Sort: Living or Nonliving

When children are comfortable with this week's sort, re-sort the pictures into groups of living and nonliving things. Set aside the cards for *sit* and *mix*. Then sort two or three of the pictures into the categories. When you pick up the next picture, invite children to identify where it will go. Continue until all the pictures have been sorted, and children are able to identify the categories.

## Day 3 — Find Words in Context

*Whole Group/Independent*

Have children re-sort their cards. Then read aloud *Fix It, Fox* with children. Have children listen for and identify any words that end with *t* or *x*. (*it, put, pot, Cat; Fix, Fox, box*) Then have children look through their picture cards to find ones whose names match pictures in the story. (*fox, box, pot*) Point out the words *fox, box,* and *pot* in the text. Reread the story, and have children hold up a card when they hear its picture name.

## Day 4 — Apply the Skill

*Independent/Partner*

Have children sort their cards again. Then have them turn to page 106 in their Word Study Notebook. Read aloud the directions, and have children identify the letters and pictures at the top of the page. Then have children work independently or with a partner to write the letters and draw pictures of things whose names end like *bat* and *ax*.

## Day 5 — Complete the Sort

*Whole Group/Independent*

### Paste in Place

Have children turn to page 105 in their Word Study Notebook. Encourage them to say the name of each word and picture at the top of the grid and listen for the ending sound. Then have them sort their cards by ending sounds and paste the pictures in place on the page.

### Play the Game

When children are finished, they may play Find the Picture. (See the Teacher Resource CD for game materials and playing directions.)

## Building Vocabulary

Children may not be familiar with the *ox* picture. Explain that an ox is a large animal that is often used on a farm to pull heavy loads or to do other hard work. Tell children that a group of these animals is called *oxen*, and that oxen can also be found in the wild.

## ESL/ELL English Language Learners

Review the picture cards with children. Ask proficient and nonproficient English speakers to work in pairs to re-sort the pictures according to the ending sounds *t* and *x*. Encourage proficient English speakers to explain the meanings of any unfamiliar words to their partner.

## Teacher Tip

To provide additional practice with ending sounds *t* and *x*, say pairs of words that end with these sounds. Tell children to stand up if both words end with the same sound and to stay seated if they do not. Use word pairs such as *fox, six; cut, ax; hot, mat;* and so on. Encourage children to name the ending sound of each word.

##  Spell Check 3

After completing Sorts 17–26, you may want to administer Spell Check 3 in the Word Study Notebook on page 149. See page 19 for instructions on progress monitoring and using the Spell Check.

# Word Families -at, -et

## Objectives

• To recognize and read words with word families -at and -et
• To identify and sort pictures and words with -at and -et

## Materials

 Big Book of Rhymes, Level K, "Wet Dog," page 57

 Teacher Resource CD, Level K, Sort 27

 Word Study Notebook, Level K, pages 107–110

 Words Their Way Library, Level K, The Wet Pet

 Teacher Resource CD, Level K, In the Pocket game

### Pictures/Words

| -at | -et |
|-----|-----|
| bat | jet |
| mat | wet |
| rat | net |
| cat | vet |

### Challenge Words

| fat | set |
|-----|-----|
| pat | met |
| sat | bet |
| flat | fret |
| brat | |

---

## Day 1 — Introduce the Sort

*Whole Group*

###  Read a Rhyme: "Wet Dog"

As you read the poem "Wet Dog," emphasize words that rhyme. *(let, bet, get, wet)* Reread the poem and have children raise their hand when they hear words that rhyme with *let. (bet, get, wet)* Help children understand that these words rhyme because they end with the same sound and letters. Read the poem again, and have children raise their hand when they hear words that end with the *-at* sound.

###  Introduce Picture/Word Sort -at, -et

Print out and cut apart the cards for Sort 27 from the Teacher Resource CD. Introduce the pictures and words, identifying *wet, net, vet,* and any others that may be unfamiliar. Demonstrate how to sort the pictures into *-at* and *-et* families. Have children describe how the names for the pictures in each column are alike. Then match each word card to its corresponding picture, and have children describe how the words in each column are alike.

## Day 2 — Practice the Sort

*Whole Group/Independent/Partner*

 You may want to begin Days 2–5 by rereading the rhyme from Day 1. Then review the previous day's sort. Help children tear out page 107 from their Word Study Notebook and cut apart the cards.

Have children work independently or with a partner to name each picture. Then, using the grid on page 109 of their Word Study Notebook, have them sort the picture cards by word families. Finally, have them read aloud each word card and match it to its corresponding picture card in each word family.

> **Alternative Sort: Alike and Different**
>
> Display all the pictures, and have children sort them by "animals" and "things." Ask why the picture for *wet* does not belong in either column. Have children then match the word cards to the pictures.

## Day 3

### Find Words in Context

*Whole Group/Independent*

Have children re-sort their cards. Then read aloud *The Wet Pet* with children. Have them listen for and identify any words that rhyme with *wet* and *pet*. Then help children look through their word cards to find *wet, jet, net,* and *pet*. Reread the book, and have children hold up the matching word card when they hear *wet, jet, net,* and *pet* in the story. Finally, have children find other words in the story that end with *-et*. *(get, vet)*

## Day 4

### Apply the Skill

*Independent/Partner*

Have children sort their cards again. Then have them turn to page 110 in their Word Study Notebook. Read aloud the directions, and have children work independently or with a partner to write the word families *-at* and *-et* and draw pictures of items that end with those letters.

## Day 5

### Complete the Sort

*Whole Group/Independent*

#### Paste in Place

Have children turn to page 109 in their Word Study Notebook. Encourage them to say the name of each word and picture at the top of the grid and listen for the ending sound. Then have children sort their picture and word cards into *-at* and *-et* word families and paste the cards in place on the page.

#### Play the Game

When children are finished, they may play In the Pocket. (See the Teacher Resource CD for game materials and playing directions.)

## Building Vocabulary

Help children realize that the word *pet* can be used to describe a thing or an action. Have children look at the *pet* picture and word in the grid on page 109, and explain that the picture shows two different meanings of *pet*. The dog in the picture is a *pet*, since he belongs to the boy; and the boy is *petting*, or stroking the hair of, the dog.

## ESL/ELL English Language Learners

Some English language learners may have difficulty differentiating between the short vowel sounds contained in the word families *-at* and *-et*. Encourage these children by modeling how to slowly elongate the vowel sound when saying each word.

## Challenge Words Activity

Encourage children to think of additional *-at* and *-et* words for you to write on blank cards. (Refer to the Challenge Words list on the facing page if necessary.) Help children read the cards. Then invite them to work in pairs or small groups to make picture cards for these new words and sort them into word families.

## Teacher Tip

Make cards showing the following letters and word families: *m, b, -at,* and *-et*. Invite children to build the word *mat* and then change one card each time to make *bat, bet,* and *met*.

73

# Word Families  -an, -en

## Objectives

- To recognize and read words with word families -an and -en
- To identify and sort pictures and words with -an and -en

## Materials

Big Book of Rhymes, Level K, "Pancakes," page 59

Teacher Resource CD, Level K, Sort 28

Word Study Notebook, Level K, pages 111–114

*Words Their Way* Library, Level K, *You Can, Too!*

Teacher Resource CD, Level K, Flip It! game

### Pictures / Words

| -an | -en |
|-----|-----|
| can | Ken |
| fan | pen |
| man | ten |
| pan | men |

### Challenge Words

| scan | den |
|------|------|
| ban | when |
| tan | then |
| ran | |

---

## Day 1  Introduce the Sort

*Whole Group*

### Read a Rhyme: "Pancakes"

As you read aloud the poem "Pancakes," emphasize words that end in the -an word family. *(pan, can)* Then reread the poem, and have children raise their hand when they hear a word ending in -an. Repeat the process with the -en word family. Point out to children that the word *again* is tricky—it ends in the -en sound, but its spelling does not end in -en.

### Introduce Picture/Word Sort -an, -en

Print out and cut apart the cards for Sort 28 from the Teacher Resource CD. Introduce the pictures and words, identifying *Ken, man, men,* and any others that may be unfamiliar. Demonstrate how to sort the pictures into -an and -en word families. Have children describe how the names for the pictures in each column are alike. *(They rhyme.)* Then match each word card to its corresponding picture, and have children describe how the words in each column are alike. *(They end in the same letters.)*

## Day 2  Practice the Sort

*Whole Group/Independent/Partner*

You may want to begin Days 2–5 by rereading the rhyme from Day 1. Then review the previous day's sort. Help children tear out page 111 from their Word Study Notebook and cut apart the cards.

Have children work independently or with a partner to name each picture. Then, using the grid on page 113 of their Word Study Notebook, have them sort the picture cards by word families. Finally, have them read aloud each word card and match it to its corresponding picture card in each word family.

### Alternative Sort: Big or Little

Re-sort the pictures and words into things that can fit in a desk and things that cannot. Set aside the cards for *ten,* and then sort two or three of the pictures into the categories. When you pick up the next picture or word card, invite children to guess where it will go. Continue to do this until all the cards have been sorted.

## Find Words in Context

*Whole Group/Independent*

Have children re-sort their cards. Then read *You Can, Too!* with children. Have them listen for and identify words that rhyme with *can*. Help children look through their picture or word cards to find the words *pan, fan,* and *can*. Have children match the cards to words in the story. Then have children find another word in the story that ends with *-an. (van)* You may want to discuss the different meanings of the word *can* in the story and the picture card *can* used in the sort.

## Apply the Skill

*Independent/Partner*

Have children sort their cards again. Then have them turn to page 114 in their Word Study Notebook. Read aloud the directions, and have children work independently or with a partner to write the word families *-an* and *-en* and draw pictures of items that end with those letters.

## Complete the Sort

*Whole Group/Independent*

### Paste in Place

Have children turn to page 113 in their Word Study Notebook. Encourage them to say the name of each word and picture at the top of the grid and listen for the ending sound. Then have children sort their picture and word cards into *-an* and *-en* word families and paste the cards in place on the page.

### Play the Game

When children are finished, they may play Flip It! (See the Teacher Resource CD for game materials and playing directions.)

## Building Vocabulary

Help children conceptualize the difference between *man* and *men* by comparing the images on the corresponding picture cards. Explain that both *man* and *men* refer to males. However, *man* is used to describe one person, while *men* is used to describe two or more people.

## ESL/ELL English Language Learners

Display the word card *Ken*, and point out the capital *K*. Tell children that *Ken* is a person's name and that a person's name always begins with a capital letter. Model sentences with the words *Ken, man,* and *men*. Then have children use the words in several sentences as they hold up the appropriate picture or word card.

## Challenge Words Activity

Encourage children to think of additional *-an* and *-en* words for you to write on blank cards. (Refer to the Challenge Words list on the facing page if necessary.) Help children read the cards. Then combine these cards with the Sort 28 word cards, and have children reread aloud and sort the cards into *-an* and *-en* word families. Guide children to reread a whole column each time a word is added to check the placement choice.

## Teacher Tip

Ongoing sorting practice can be encouraged by displaying large outline drawings of a can and a hen with the picture or word cards. Children can place cards appropriately to "fill the can" and "feed the hen" with rhyming words.

You may wish to use the Sort 28 **Build, Blend, and Extend**. (See the Teacher Resource CD.)

# Word Families -ig, -og

## Objectives

- To recognize and read words with word families *-ig* and *-og*
- To identify and sort pictures and words with *-ig* and *-og*

## Materials

 Big Book of Rhymes, Level K, "Big Frog," page 61

 Teacher Resource CD, Level K, Sort 29

 Word Study Notebook, Level K, pages 115–118

 *Words Their Way* Library, Level K, *A Pig in a Wig*

 Teacher Resource CD, Level K, Go Fish game

### Pictures/Words

| -ig | -og |
|-----|-----|
| twig | log |
| wig | dog |
| jig | jog |
| pig | fog |

### Challenge Words

| fig | smog |
|-----|------|
| rig | hog |
| big | clog |

## Day 1 — Introduce the Sort

*Whole Group*

 ### Read a Rhyme: "Big Frog"

Read aloud the poem "Big Frog" several times, emphasizing the rhyming words. *(frog, log; big, twig)*. Then ask children to name words they hear in the poem that rhyme. Help children understand that these words rhyme because they end with the same sound and letters. Read the poem again, omitting the last word of the first four lines, and have children supply the missing word.

 ### Introduce Picture/Word Sort *-ig, -og*

Print out and cut apart the cards for Sort 29 from the Teacher Resource CD. Introduce the pictures and words, identifying *jig, fog, jog,* and any others that may be unfamiliar. Demonstrate how to sort the pictures into *-ig* and *-og* word families. Have children describe how the names for the pictures in each column are alike. *(They rhyme.)* Then match each word card to its corresponding picture, and have children describe how the words in each column are alike. *(They end in the same letters.)*

## Day 2 — Practice the Sort

*Whole Group/Independent/Partner*

 You may want to begin Days 2–5 by rereading the rhyme from Day 1. Then review the previous day's sort. Help children tear out page 115 from their Word Study Notebook and cut apart the cards.

Have children work independently or with a partner to name each picture. Then, using the grid on page 117 of their Word Study Notebook, have them sort the picture cards by word families. Finally, have them read aloud each word card and match it to its corresponding picture card in each word family.

### Alternative Sort: Animals or Action

Lead children to sort the pictures by animals *(dog, pig)* and actions *(jig, jog)*. Remind children that an action is a movement, or what something can do. Then ask children to invent a new category for the picture cards that don't fall into either category. *(things)* Have children then match the word cards to the pictures.

## Day 3 · Find Words in Context

*Whole Group/Independent*

Have children re-sort their cards. Then read aloud *A Pig in a Wig* with children. Have them listen for and identify words that rhyme with *pig*. Then have children look through their cards to find the picture and word cards for *pig*. Reread the book, and have children hold up the cards when the word is used in the story.

## Day 4 · Apply the Skill

*Independent/Partner*

Have children sort their cards again. Then have them turn to page 118 in their Word Study Notebook. Read aloud the directions, and have children work independently or with a partner to write the word families *-ig* and *-og* and draw pictures of items that end with those letters.

## Day 5 · Complete the Sort

*Whole Group/Independent*

### Paste in Place

Have children turn to page 117 in their Word Study Notebook. Encourage them to say the name of each word and picture at the top of the grid and listen for the ending sound. Then have children sort their picture and word cards into *-ig* and *-og* word families and paste the cards in place on the page.

### Play the Game

When children are finished, they may play Go Fish. (See the Teacher Resource CD for playing cards and directions.)

## Building Vocabulary

If children are unfamiliar with the word *jig*, have them try to discern its meaning by examining the image on the corresponding picture card. Help them understand that a jig is a dance with kicking and jumping.

## English Language Learners

The similar words *jig* and *jog* may need reinforcement. Have children say each word aloud, making sure they pronounce all the sounds. Then say and act out a sentence for each word, and have children copy you. Clarify the word *twig* and its picture by pointing out a real twig on a branch.

## Challenge Words Activity

Encourage children to find or think of additional *-ig* and *-og* words for you to write on blank cards. (Refer to the Challenge Words list on the facing page if necessary.) Help children read the cards. Then combine these cards with the Sort 29 word cards, and have children reread aloud and sort the cards into *-ig* and *-og* word families. Guide children to reread a whole column each time a word is added to check the placement choice. To reinforce meaning, children can also make a picture card for each Challenge Word and then match all picture cards to word cards.

## Teacher Tip

Connect to science with the word *fog*. Discuss the differences among fog, rain, and snow. Then find or draw pictures of these weather elements and explore why windows can become fogged.

You may wish to use the Sort 29 **Build, Blend, and Extend**. (See the Teacher Resource CD.)

# Word Families  -in, -un

## Objectives

- To recognize and read words with word families *-in* and *-un*
- To identify and sort pictures and words with *-in* and *-un*

## Materials

 Big Book of Rhymes, Level K, "Fun in the Sun," page 63

 Teacher Resource CD, Level K, Sort 30

 Word Study Notebook, Level K, pages 119–122

 *Words Their Way* Library, Level K, *Pin It!*

 Teacher Resource CD, Level K, At the Beach game

### Pictures/Words

| -in | -un |
|------|------|
| twin | fun |
| pin | sun |
| bin | run |
| chin | bun |

### Challenge Words

| tin | spun |
|------|------|
| shin | stun |
| spin | pun |
| thin | |

---

## Day 1 — Introduce the Sort

*Whole Group*

 **Read a Rhyme: "Fun in the Sun"**

As you read aloud the poem "Fun in the Sun," have children make a sun with their hands when they hear a word that rhymes with *sun* (*fun*) and point to their chin when they hear a word that rhymes with *chin* (*skin*). Help children understand that the words rhyme because they end with the same sound and letters. Read the poem again, omitting the last word of each line, and have children supply the missing word.

 **Introduce Picture/Word Sort -in, -un**

Print out and cut apart the cards for Sort 30 from the Teacher Resource CD. Introduce the pictures and words, identifying *bin, bun, run,* and any others that may be unfamiliar. Demonstrate how to sort the pictures into *-in* and *-un* word families. Have children describe how the names for the pictures in each column are alike. Then match each word card to its corresponding picture, and have children describe how the words in each column are alike.

## Day 2 — Practice the Sort

*Whole Group/Independent/Partner*

 You may want to begin Days 2–5 by rereading the rhyme from Day 1. Then review the previous day's sort. Help children tear out page 119 from their Word Study Notebook and cut apart the cards.

Have children work independently or with a partner to name each picture. Then, using the grid on page 121 of their Word Study Notebook, have them sort the picture cards by word families. Finally, have them read aloud each word card and match it to its corresponding picture card in each word family.

> **Alternative Sort: What Goes In?**
>
> Provide a bin that children will use to re-sort the word and picture cards. Tell children that only cards that rhyme with *-in* will go in the bin; the other cards will be placed beside it. Stack the cards facedown, and have children take turns drawing one. Ask "Does your card go *in*?" and have the child use the word in a sentence or tell what the word means before placing the card in the appropriate location.

## Find Words in Context

*Whole Group/Independent*

Have children re-sort their cards. Then read *Pin It!* with children. Have them listen for and identify words that rhyme with *pin*. Then help children look through their word cards to find the words *chin* and *pin*. Have children match the word cards with words in the text. Then have children find other words that end with *in*. (spin, win)

## Apply the Skill

*Independent/Partner*

Have children sort their cards again. Then have them turn to page 122 in their Word Study Notebook. Read aloud the directions, and have children work independently or with a partner to write the word families *-in* and *-un* and draw pictures of items that end with those letters.

## Complete the Sort

*Whole Group/Independent*

### Paste in Place

Have children turn to page 121 in their Word Study Notebook. Encourage them to say the name of each word and picture at the top of the grid and listen for the ending sound. Then have children sort their picture and word cards into *-in* and *-un* word families and paste the cards in place on the page.

### Play the Game

When children are finished, they may play *At the Beach*. (See the Teacher Resource CD for game materials and playing directions.)

## Building Vocabulary

Tell children that the word *bun* can have different meanings, depending on how it is used. Display the picture card for *bun*, and ask children to tell what the word means in this instance. *(a round roll)* Then ask children how they might use the word *bun* to describe someone's hair. Lead them to the realization that the word can also describe hair that is pulled back into a ball or knot.

## ESL/ELL English Language Learners

To help children learn to distinguish between the *-in* and *-un* word families, say two words from Sort 30 (such as *bin* and *bun*). Elongate each vowel sound. Have children repeat the words after you in the same way and tell whether the words have the same ending sound. Repeat with other word pairs, making sure to include words with both similar and different endings in the pairs.

## Challenge Words Activity

Encourage children to think of additional *-in* and *-un* words for you to write on blank cards. (Refer to the Challenge Words list on the facing page if necessary.) Help children read the cards. Then combine these cards with the Sort 30 word cards, and have children reread aloud and sort the cards into *-in* and *-un* word families. Guide children to reread a whole column each time a word is added to check the placement choice.

## Teacher Tip

Make cards showing the following letters and word families: *b, f, -in,* and *-un*. Invite children to build the word *bin* and then change one card each time to make *fin, fun,* and *bun*.

# Word Families  -at, -et, -ut

## Objectives

- To recognize and read words with word families -at, -et, and -ut
- To identify and sort pictures and words with -at, -et, and -ut

## Materials

 Big Book of Rhymes, Level K, "A Pet, Please," page 65

 Teacher Resource CD, Level K, Sort 31

 Word Study Notebook, Level K, pages 123–126

 Words Their Way Library, Level K, A Cat and a Hat

 Teacher Resource CD, Level K, Find the Picture game

### Pictures/Words

| -at | -et | -ut |
|-----|-----|-----|
| cat | net | cut |
| mat | jet | nut |
| bat | met | rut |
| rat | wet | hut |

### Challenge Words

| brat | bet | but |
|------|-----|-----|
| chat | let | gut |
| scat | fret | jut |

---

## Day 1 — Introduce the Sort

*Whole Group*

 **Read a Rhyme: "A Pet, Please"**

Read aloud the poem "A Pet, Please." Then as you reread the title and the poem, have children raise their hand when they hear the words *pet, cat,* and *but.* Point out the ending in each word. Then reread the first two lines to have children identify a word that ends the same way that *pet* does. *(get)* Reread lines 3 and 4 to have children find a rhyming words for *cat. (bat)* Read the poem once more, omitting some target words, and invite children to supply them.

 **Introduce Picture/Word Sort -at, -et, -ut**

Print out and cut apart the cards for Sort 31 from the Teacher Resource CD. Introduce the pictures and words, identifying *mat, met, rut,* and any others that may be unfamiliar. Demonstrate how to sort the pictures into -at, -et, and -ut word families. Have children describe how the names for the pictures in each column are alike. Then match each word card to its corresponding picture, and have children describe how the words in each column are alike.

## Day 2 — Practice the Sort

*Whole Group/Independent/Partner*

 You may want to begin Days 2–5 by rereading the rhyme from Day 1. Then review the previous day's sort. Help children tear out page 123 from their Word Study Notebook and cut apart the cards.

Have children work independently or with a partner to name each picture. Then, using the grid on page 125 of their Word Study Notebook, have them sort the picture cards by word families. Finally, have them read aloud each word card and match it to its corresponding picture card in each word family.

> **Alternative Sort: Guess My Category**
> Challenge children to figure out how you are re-sorting certain words. Display all the word cards and model choosing two that begin alike at a time, such as *cat* and *cut* or *mat* and *met.* When children can tell what you are doing, let them finish pairing the words *(net, nut; rat, rut)* and make a column of the words that do not form a pair *(bat, jet, wet, hut).*

## Find Words in Context

*Whole Group*

Have children re-sort their cards. Then read *A Cat and a Hat* with children. Have them listen for and identify *cat* and other words that rhyme with *cat* as each page is read. Reread each page, having children echo read after you. Then have children find and point out the words *cat, mat, bat, rat,* and *hat.*

**Day**
**4**

## Apply the Skill

*Independent/Partner*

Have children sort their cards again. Then have them turn to page 126 in their Word Study Notebook. Read aloud the directions, and have children work independently or with a partner to write the word families *-at, -et,* and *-ut* and draw pictures of items that end with those letters.

**Day**
**5**

## Complete the Sort

*Whole Group/Independent*

### Paste in Place

Have children turn to page 125 in their Word Study Notebook. Encourage them to say the name of each word and picture at the top of the grid and listen for the ending sound. Then have children sort their picture and word cards into *-at, -et,* and *-ut* word families and paste the cards in place on the page.

### Play the Game

When children are finished, they may play Find the Picture. (See the Teacher Resource CD for game materials and playing directions.)

## Building Vocabulary

Define in context the word *met* by explaining that it describes an action that happened in the past. Have children describe the *met* image in the corresponding picture card, and lead them to the determination that *met* means "came face to face with."

## ESL/ELL English Language Learners

Ensure that children hear and say the final *t* sounds in *-at, -et,* and *-ut* words. If necessary, repeat responses of words and sentences slowly and very distinctly. Have children hold a hand in front of their mouth as they speak each word, and discuss how to form each sound with breath, tongue, and mouth.

## Challenge Words Activity

Encourage children to think of additional *-at, -et,* and *-ut* words for you to write on blank cards. (Refer to the Challenge Words list on the facing page if necessary.) Help children read the cards. Then combine these cards with the Sort 31 word cards, and have children reread aloud and sort the cards into *-at, -et,* and *-ut* word families. Guide children to reread a whole column each time a word is added to check the placement choice.

## Teacher Tip

Make a word with newly introduced *-ut* especially memorable. Begin a poster of "Things That Are Cut" with a short discussion. Invite children to add drawings of materials that are cut, along with drawings of scissors, a saw, a table knife, a paper cutter, and other cutting tools.

You may wish to use the Sort 31 **Build, Blend, and Extend**. (See the Teacher Resource CD.)

# Word Families  -an, -en, -in, -un

## Objectives

- To recognize and read words with word families -an, -en, -in, and -un
- To identify and sort pictures and words with -an, -en, -in, and -un

## Materials

Big Book of Rhymes, Level K, "Grand Slam," page 67

Teacher Resource CD, Level K, Sort 36

Word Study Notebook, Level K, pages 127–130

*Words Their Way* Library, Level K, *The Merry-Go-Round*

Teacher Resource CD, Level K, Home Run! game

### Pictures/Words

| -an | -en | -in | -un |
|-----|-----|-----|-----|
| fan | men | twin | run |
| pan | pen | pin | bun |

### Challenge Words

| ban | den | shin | fun |
|------|------|------|------|
| can | ten | bin | pun |
| scan | then | spin | spun |

---

**Day 1**

## Introduce the Sort

*Whole Group*

### Read a Rhyme: "Grand Slam"

Read "Grand Slam," and have children raise their hand when you get to a word that rhymes with *fun*. Demonstrate what the ending -an sounds like, and ask children to identify a word containing the ending during another read of the poem. Continue by demonstrating -en and -in and asking children to find those words as you reread the poem.

### Introduce Picture/Word Sort -an, -en, -in, -un

Print out and cut apart the cards for Sort 32 from the Teacher Resource CD. Introduce the pictures and words, identifying *fan, twin, run*, and any others that may be unfamiliar. Demonstrate how to sort the pictures into -an, -en, -in, and -un word families. Then match each word card to its corresponding picture, and have children describe how the words in each column are alike. (*They end in the same letters.*)

**Day 2**

## Practice the Sort

*Whole Group/Independent/Partner*

You may want to begin Days 2–5 by rereading the rhyme from Day 1. Then review the previous day's sort. Help children tear out page 127 from their Word Study Notebook and cut apart the cards.

Have children work independently or with a partner to name each picture. Then, using the grid on page 129 of their Word Study Notebook, have them sort the picture cards by word families. Finally, have them read aloud each word card and match it to its corresponding picture card in each word family.

### Alternative Sort: Guess My Category

Display all the pictures, and have children first place the people *(men, twin)* in a column. Then begin to make a column of "Things People Can Hold," without telling the category. Continue until children guess the category and can take over building the column. Ask why the picture for *run* does not belong in either column.

## Day 3
## Find Words in Context

*Whole Group*

Have children re-sort their cards. Then write *van*, *bin*, and *fun* as column headers on the chalkboard or chart paper and read the words. Tell children to listen for words that rhyme with these words as you read aloud *The Merry-Go-Round*. Have children recall rhyming words from the book to list. Reread each page, having children echo read after you and point out rhyming words for the columns. Then have children search the book and point out the words *ran*, *in*, *spin*, *run*, and *spun*.

## Day 4
## Apply the Skill

*Independent/Partner*

Have children sort their cards again. Then have them turn to page 130 in their Word Study Notebook. Read aloud the directions, and have children work independently or with a partner to write the word families *-an*, *-en*, *-in*, and *-un* and draw pictures of items that end with those letters.

## Day 5
## Complete the Sort

*Whole Group/Independent*

### Paste in Place

Have children turn to page 129 in their Word Study Notebook. Encourage them to say the name of each word and picture at the top of the grid and listen for the ending sound. Then have children sort their picture and word cards into *-an*, *-en*, *-in*, and *-un* word families and paste the cards in place on the page.

### Play the Game

When children are finished, they may play Home Run! (See the Teacher Resource CD for game materials and playing directions.)

## Building Vocabulary

Explain that the word *fan* can describe both a thing and an action. Have children look at the picture card for *fan* and determine whether it shows a thing or an action. Then pantomime fanning yourself, and ask children to describe what you are doing. Point out that in this case, *fan* is an action word.

## ESL/ELL English Language Learners

If children have trouble pronouncing a few words, work with two word families at a time. Each day, include one word family that is challenging and one with which children are very successful.

## Challenge Words Activity

Encourage children to think of additional *-an*, *-en*, *-in*, and *-un* words for you to write on blank cards. (Refer to the Challenge Words list on the facing page if necessary.) Help children read the cards. Then combine these cards with the Sort 32 word cards, and have children reread aloud and sort the cards into *-an*, *-en*, *-in*, and *-un* word families. Guide children to reread a whole column each time a word is added to check the placement choice.

## Teacher Tip

Provide *f*, *p*, *t*, *-an*, *-en*, *-in*, and *-un* cards for each child. Use the words *fan-fin-fun* to show how children can make a word and then change one card each time to make two other words. Repeat the activity with the word groups *pan*, *pen*, *pin*; *tan*, *ten*, *tin*; *fan*, *pan*, *tan*; and *fin*, *pin*, *tin*.

 ## Spell Check 4

After completing Sorts 27–32, you may want to administer Spell Check 4 in the Word Study Notebook on page 150. See page 19 for instructions on progress monitoring and using the Spell Check.

# Short Vowels  a, i

## Objectives

- To identify short *a* and *i* vowel sounds
- To identify and sort pictures with the short vowel sounds *a* and *i*

## Materials

 Big Book of Rhymes, Level K, "This and That," page 69

 Teacher Resource CD, Level K, Sort 33

 Word Study Notebook, Level K, pages 131–134

 *Words Their Way* Library, Level K, *A Fin, a Grin, and a Pin*

 Teacher Resource CD, Level K, Match! game

### Pictures

| a | i |
|------|-------|
| cat | mill |
| rat | pig |
| bag | six |
| wag | twins |
| map | pit |
| cap | wig |

### Challenge Words

| | |
|------|------|
| can | rip |
| cab | bit |
| jam | win |
| ham | him |
| fan | fig |

---

## Day 1 Introduce the Sort

*Whole Group*

 **Read a Rhyme: "This and That"**

As you read the poem "This and That," emphasize words that contain short *a* and *i* sounds. *(that, glad, have, and, gigantic; this, is, skin, chin, big, grin)* Reread the poem, and ask children to raise their hand when they hear words that contain the short *a* sound. Repeat the procedure for short *i*. Then say the words from the poem that contain each short vowel sound, and have children say them after you.

 **Introduce Picture Sort Short Vowels *a, i***

Print out and cut apart the cards for Sort 33 from the Teacher Resource CD. Identify *mill, bag, cap,* and any other pictures that may be unfamiliar. Then demonstrate how to sort the pictures by short *a* and short *i* sounds. Have children name the pictures in each column and identify how they are alike and different.

## Day 2 Practice the Sort

*Whole Group/Independent/Partner*

 You may want to begin Days 2–5 by rereading the rhyme from Day 1. Then review the previous day's sort. Help children tear out page 131 from their Word Study Notebook and cut apart the cards.

Have children work independently or with a partner to say the name of each picture and, using the grid on page 133 of their Word Study Notebook, sort the picture cards by short *a* and short *i* sounds.

> **Alternative Sort: On a Trip**
>
> Re-sort the pictures into things children might take on a trip and things they would not. Set aside the pictures for *wag* and *six*. Then show children the pictures one at a time, and have them put each picture in the appropriate category. Encourage children to explain their thinking as they sort the pictures.

## 3 Find Words in Context

*Whole Group*

Have children re-sort their cards. Then read aloud *A Fin, a Grin, and a Pin* with children. Have children raise their hand each time they hear a word with the short *a* sound. *(that, has, and)* Reread the story, and have children raise their hand each time they hear a word with the short *i* sound. *(fin, grin, pin, fish)*

Day

## 4 Apply the Skill

*Independent/Partner*

Have children sort their cards again. Then have them turn to page 134 in their Word Study Notebook. Read aloud the directions, and have children identify the pictures on the page. Then have children work independently or with a partner to write the short vowel (*a* or *i*) that completes each name.

Day

## 5 Complete the Sort

*Whole Group/Independent*

### Paste in Place

Have children turn to page 133 in their Word Study Notebook. Encourage them to say the words and name the pictures at the top of the grid, listening for the short vowel sounds. Then have them sort their pictures by short *a* and short *i* sounds and paste the pictures in place on the page.

### Play the Game

When children are finished, they may play Match! (See the Teacher Resource CD for game materials and playing directions.)

## Building Vocabulary

You may want to define in context the word *mill* for children. Explain that a mill is a place where wheat, wood, and other items are ground or crushed up. It is also often used as another word for *factory*.

## ESL/ELL English Language Learners

Review the pictures with children. Emphasize animal names that contain short *a* or *i* sounds (*cat, rat, pig*) by acting out the behavior or attributes associated with each animal. Have children mimic your actions as they pronounce the animal names.

## Challenge Words Activity

Challenge children to think of other short *a* and short *i* words. (Refer to the Challenge Words list on the facing page, if necessary.) Help children make word cards for the words, and then have them work in small groups to sort the words into short *a* and short *i* categories.

## Teacher Tip

If some of the children complete their sort early, suggest that they check their work. Then pair them with other children to act as helpers by answering questions and sharing tips.

# Short Vowels o, u

## Objectives

- To identify short o and u vowel sounds
- To identify and sort pictures with the short vowel sounds o and u

## Materials

Big Book of Rhymes, Level K, "Soup's Ready!," page 71

Teacher Resource CD, Level K, Sort 34

Word Study Notebook, Level K, pages 135–138

*Words Their Way* Library, Level K, *What Is Hot?*

Teacher Resource CD, Level K, Sip the Soup! game

### Pictures

| o | u |
|-----|-----|
| top | bug |
| pot | sun |
| cot | mug |
| mop | nut |
| rock | cut |
| box | rug |

### Challenge Words

| mom | but |
|-----|-----|
| job | tub |
| hop | hum |
| lot | rub |
| not | pup |

---

## Day 1 — Introduce the Sort

*Whole Group*

### Read a Rhyme: "Soup's Ready!"

Introduce the sounds of short o and u vowels by reading aloud the poem "Soup's Ready!" As you read, emphasize the words that contain short o and u sounds. *(hot, on, top; yum, up, cup)* Reread the poem, and ask children to raise their hand when they hear words that contain the short o sound. Repeat the procedure for short u. Then say the words from the poem that contain each short vowel sound and have children say them after you.

### Introduce Picture Sort Short Vowels o, u

Print out and cut apart the cards for Sort 34 from the Teacher Resource CD. Introduce the pictures, identifying *cot, rock, top,* and any others that may be unfamiliar. Then demonstrate how to sort the pictures by short o and short u sounds. Have children name the pictures in each column and tell how they are alike and different.

## Day 2 — Practice the Sort

*Whole Group/Independent/Partner*

You may want to begin Days 2–5 by rereading the rhyme from Day 1. Then review the previous day's sort. Help children tear out page 135 from their Word Study Notebook and cut apart the cards.

Have children work independently or with a partner to say the name of each picture and, using the grid on page 137 of their Word Study Notebook, sort the picture cards by short o and short u sounds.

### Alternative Sort: Moving Along

Re-sort the pictures into groups of things that can and cannot move. Begin by sorting two or three of the pictures into the categories. When you pick up the next picture, invite children to guess where it will go. Continue until all the pictures have been sorted. Encourage children to explain their reasoning.

## 3 Find Words in Context

*Whole Group/Independent*

Have children re-sort their cards. Then read aloud the book *What Is Hot?* Have children raise their hand each time they hear a word with the short *o* sound. *(hot, not, pot)* Reread the story, and have children raise their hand each time they hear a word with the short *u* sound. *(sun)* Then have children look through their picture cards and find the two that match a picture in the book. *(sun, pot)*

**Day**
## 4 Apply the Skill

*Independent/Partner*

Have children sort their cards again. Then have them turn to page 138 in their Word Study Notebook. Read aloud the directions, and have children identify the pictures on the page. Then have children work independently or with a partner to write the short vowel *(o or u)* that completes each name.

**Day**
## 5 Complete the Sort

*Whole Group/Independent*

### Paste in Place

Have children turn to page 137 in their Word Study Notebook. Encourage them to say the words and name the pictures at the top of the grid, listening for the short vowel sounds. Then have them sort their pictures by short *o* and short *u* sounds and paste the pictures in place on the page.

### Play the Game

When children are finished, they may play Sip the Soup! (See the Teacher Resource CD for game materials and playing directions.)

## Building Vocabulary

Children may refer to the *cot* picture card as a *bed*. Explain that a cot is a type of bed, but that it is usually much narrower than a regular bed and can often be folded up. Encourage children to describe a cot they've seen or an experience they've had sleeping on a cot.

## ESL/ELL English Language Learners

Place the picture cards faceup on a table and review their names. Then create short vowel riddles, such as: "Say the picture name that contains the sound of short *u* and names something you can drink from" *(mug)* or "Say two picture names that contain the sound of short *o* and can be found in a kitchen." *(pot, mop)*

## Challenge Words Activity

Challenge children to think of other short *o* and short *u* words. (Refer to the Challenge Words list on the facing page, if necessary.) Help children make word cards for the words, and then have them work in small groups to sort the words into short *o* and short *u* categories.

## Teacher Tip

Encourage children to create their own picture cards for words that contain short *o* and short *u* vowel sounds. Have them share their pictures with each other.

# Sort 35

# Short Vowels a, e, i

## Objectives

- To identify short *a*, *e*, and *i* vowel sounds
- To identify and sort pictures with the short vowel sounds *a*, *e*, and *i*

## Materials

Big Book of Rhymes, Level K, "Duck and Cat," page 73

Teacher Resource CD, Level K, Sort 35

Word Study Notebook, Level K, pages 139–142

*Words Their Way* Library, Level K, *What Can Quack?*

Teacher Resource CD, Level K, Who Can Quack? game

| Pictures | | |
|---|---|---|
| *a* | *e* | *i* |
| bat | net | brick |
| rag | beg | pit |
| pad | men | hill |
| dad | leg | pig |
| flag | bed | ship |

| Challenge Words | | |
|---|---|---|
| lad | yes | hid |
| fan | sell | mix |
| yam | peg | zip |
| dam | get | big |
| lap | fell | lit |

## Day 1 — Introduce the Sort

*Whole Group*

### Read a Rhyme: "Duck and Cat"

As you read aloud "Duck and Cat," emphasize the words that contain short *a*, *e*, and *i* sounds. *(cat, can, quack, answer, back; steps; grin)* Explain that *cat* contains the short *a* sound and *grin* contains the short *i* sound, while *steps* contains the short *e* sound. Read the poem again, and encourage children to quack each time they hear a word that contains the short *a* sound. Repeat the procedure for short *e* and short *i*.

### Introduce Picture Sort
### Short Vowels *a, e, i*

Print out and cut apart the picture cards for Sort 35 from the Teacher Resource CD. Introduce the pictures, identifying *beg, pit, pad,* and any others that may be unfamiliar. Then demonstrate how to sort the pictures by short *a*, short *e*, and short *i* sounds. Have children name the pictures in each column and describe how they are alike and different.

## Day 2 — Practice the Sort

*Whole Group/Independent/Partner*

You may want to begin Days 2–5 by rereading the rhyme from Day 1. Then review the previous day's sort. Help children tear out page 139 from their Word Study Notebook and cut apart the cards.

Have children work independently or with a partner to say the name of each picture and, using the grid on page 141 of their Word Study Notebook, sort the picture cards by the short vowel sounds *a*, *e*, and *i*.

### Alternative Sort: Water Sort

When children are comfortable with this week's sort, ask them to think about which pictures have something to do with water and which do not. Sort two or three of the pictures into the categories. When you pick up the next picture, invite children to tell where it will go. Continue until all the pictures have been sorted. Encourage children to explain their reasoning.

88

## Day 3 — Find Words in Context

*Whole Group/Independent*

Have children re-sort their cards. Then read aloud *What Can Quack?* with children. Have children listen for and identify any words that include the short vowel sounds *a* or *i*. (*What, can, quack, cat; quilt*) Encourage them to make their own picture cards using the short *a* and *i* words in the story.

## Day 4 — Apply the Skill

*Independent/Partner*

Have children sort their cards again. Then have them turn to page 142 in their Word Study Notebook. Read aloud the directions, and have children identify the pictures on the page. Then have children work independently or with a partner to write the short vowel (*a*, *e*, or *i*) that completes each name.

## Day 5 — Complete the Sort

*Whole Group/Independent*

### Paste in Place

Have children turn to page 141 in their Word Study Notebook. Encourage them to say the words and name the pictures at the top of the grid, listening for the short vowel sounds. Then have them sort their pictures by short *a*, *e*, and *i* sounds and paste the pictures in place on the page.

### Play the Game

When children are finished, they may play Who Can Quack? (See the Teacher Resource CD for game materials and playing directions.)

## Building Vocabulary

Children may have trouble identifying the *beg* picture card. Ask them if they've ever seen a dog behave like the one in the picture, and why they think a dog might behave that way. Lead children to the determination that the dog in the picture is asking for something it wants. Explain that the word for this is *beg*.

## ESL/ELL English Language Learners

Set aside the picture card for *beg*. Then review the picture names with children. Make sure children understand each picture name by asking them to explain where each might be found. Model the activity by holding up the picture of *ship* and explaining that ships are found in water. Hold up successive picture cards, and encourage children to list places where they might be found.

## Challenge Words Activity

Challenge children to think of other short *a*, short *e*, and short *i* words. (Refer to the Challenge Words list on the facing page, if necessary.) Help children make word cards for the words, and then have them work in small groups to sort the words into short *a*, short *e*, and short *i* categories.

## Teacher Tip

Encourage children to pursue sorting activities in small groups. Pair lower-level students with higher-level students in order to foster cooperative learning skills.

# Short Vowels  a, e, i, o, u

## Objectives

- To identify short *a*, *e*, *i*, *o*, and *u* vowel sounds
- To identify and sort pictures with the short vowel sounds *a*, *e*, *i*, *o*, and *u*

## Materials

 Big Book of Rhymes, Level K, "We Love Pizza!," page 75

 Teacher Resource CD, Level K, Sort 36

 Word Study Notebook, Level K, pages 143–146

 *Words Their Way* Library, Level K, *Pat's Perfect Pizza*

 Teacher Resource CD, Level K, Pizza Party game

### Pictures

| a | e | i | o | u |
|---|---|---|---|---|
| hat | pet | sit | hot | sun |
| nap | desk | ship | box | cut |
| pad | web | six | sock | rug |
| mat | peg | mill | mop | run |

### Challenge Words

| ran | bell | miss | top | bud |
|---|---|---|---|---|
| wag | tell | kit | jot | hub |
| nag | bet | pit | mob | jug |
| ram | fed | rid | lot | fun |

## Day 1 — Introduce the Sort

*Whole Group*

 **Read a Rhyme: "We Love Pizza!"**

As you read aloud the poem "We Love Pizza!," emphasize the words that contain short *a*, *e*, *i*, *o*, or *u* sounds. (*bathtub, can't, van, can; den, wherever; in, kitchen; shop, stop; bathtub*) Reread the poem, and ask children to raise their hand when they hear a word that contains the short *a*, *e*, *i*, *o*, or *u* sound. Then say the words that contain short vowel sounds, and have children say them after you.

 **Introduce Picture Sort
Short Vowels *a, e, i, o, u***

Print out and cut apart the picture cards for Sort 36 from the Teacher Resource CD. Introduce the pictures, identifying *peg, run, ten,* and any others that may be unfamiliar. Then demonstrate how to sort the pictures by short *a, e, i, o,* and *u* vowel sounds. Have children name the pictures in each column and describe how they are alike and different.

## Day 2 — Practice the Sort

*Whole Group/Independent/Partner*

 You may want to begin Days 2–5 by rereading the rhyme from Day 1. Then review the previous day's sort. Help children tear out page 143 from their Word Study Notebook and cut apart the cards.

Have children work independently or with a partner to say the name of each picture and, using the grid on page 145 of their Word Study Notebook, sort the picture cards by short *a, e, i, o,* and *u* sounds.

### Alternative Sort: Actions or Things

When children are comfortable with this week's sort, re-sort the pictures into actions and things. Set aside the card for *six*. Then begin by sorting two or three of the pictures into the categories. When you pick up the next picture, invite children to tell where it will go. Continue until all the cards have been sorted.

## Day 3 — Find Words in Context

*Whole Group*

Have children re-sort their cards. Then read aloud *Pat's Perfect Pizza* with children. Have children listen for and identify any words that include the short *a, e, i, o,* or *u* sounds. Then reread the story, stopping to ask children to determine which short vowel sounds are represented by specific words.

## Day 4 — Apply the Skill

*Independent/Partner*

Have children sort their cards again. Then have them turn to page 146 in their Word Study Notebook. Read aloud the directions, and have children identify the pictures on the page. Then have children work independently or with a partner to write the short vowel *(a, e, i, o,* or *u)* that completes each name.

## Day 5 — Complete the Sort

*Whole Group/Independent*

### Paste in Place

Have children turn to page 145 in their Word Study Notebook. Encourage them to say the words and name the pictures at the top of the grid, listening for the short vowel sounds. Then have them sort their pictures by short *a, e, i, o,* and *u* sounds and paste the pictures in place on the page.

### Play the Game

When children are finished, they may play Pizza Party. (See the Teacher Resource CD for game materials and playing directions.)

## Building Vocabulary

If children have trouble identifying the picture for *peg*, define the word in the context of the picture: a small piece of wood used to hold things together, plug up an opening, or hang things on. Discuss with children where in their classroom or homes they might find a peg.

## ESL/ELL English Language Learners

Review the pictures with children and have them say each picture name. Listen to confirm that children are able to clearly distinguish between the short *a, e, i, o,* and *u* vowel sounds.

## Challenge Words Activity

Challenge children to think of other short *a*, short *e*, short *i*, short *o*, and short *u* words. (Refer to the Challenge Words list on the facing page, if necessary.) Help children make word cards for the words, and then have them work in small groups to sort the words into short *a*, short *e*, short *i*, short *o*, and short *u* categories.

## Teacher Tip

Upon completion of each sort, encourage children to name other words that contain the short *a, e, i, o,* or *u* sounds.

 ## Spell Check 5

After completing Sorts 33–36, you may want to administer Spell Check 5 in the Word Study Notebook on page 151. See page 19 for instructions on progress monitoring and using the Spell Check.